▼ ▼ ▼

LEAVING WITHOUT LOSING

THE WAR ON TERROR
AFTER IRAQ AND AFGHANISTAN

MARK N. KATZ

The Johns Hopkins University Press *Baltimore*

Johns Hopkins Paperback edition, 2013
2 4 6 8 9 7 5 3 1

The Johns Hopkins University Press
2715 North Charles Street
Baltimore, Maryland 21218-4363
www.press.jhu.edu

*The Library of Congress has cataloged the hardcover edition
of this book as follows:*
Katz, Mark N.
Leaving without losing : the War on Terror after Iraq and
Afghanistan / Mark N. Katz.
p. cm.
Includes bibliographical references and index.
ISBN-13: 978-1-4214-0558-2 (hdbk. : alk. paper)
ISBN-13: 978-1-4214-0588-9 (electronic)
ISBN-10: 1-4214-0558-X (hdbk. : alk. paper)
ISBN-10: 1-4214-0588-1 (electronic)
1. War on Terrorism, 2001–2009. 2. Terrorism—
Prevention. 3. Afghan War, 2001– . 4. Iraq War, 2003– .
5. United States—History, Military—21st century.
6. United States—Foreign relations—21st century. I. Title.
HV6432.K37 2012
363.325'160973—dc23   2011036012

A catalog record for this book is available from the
British Library.

ISBN-13: 978-1-4214-1183-5
ISBN-10: 1-4214-1183-0

*Special discounts are available for bulk purchases of this book. For
more information, please contact Special Sales at 410-516-6936
or specialsales@press.jhu.edu.*

The Johns Hopkins University Press uses environmentally
friendly book materials, including recycled text paper that is
composed of at least 30 percent post-consumer waste,
whenever possible.

Leaving without Losing

To my mother,
Eithne Dolores Dorney

Contents

Acknowledgments

I am grateful to several individuals and institutions for facilitating and encouraging the writing of this book. George Mason University granted me a sabbatical during the Fall 2010 semester, which allowed me the necessary time for research and writing. The Middle East Policy Council in Washington, D.C., generously provided me with an office and an exceptionally warm and friendly atmosphere in which to carry out my research and write the initial draft. I would like to thank everyone there for being so helpful to me, especially Frank R. Anderson (the Council's president), Thomas R. Mattair (its executive director), and Anne Joyce (editor of the Council's journal, *Middle East Policy*).

Thanks are also due to the Middle East Policy Council for hosting a breakfast seminar for me on November 30, 2010, in which I discussed this project with a small, highly knowledgeable group. In addition, I am grateful to the Middle East Institute—especially its vice president, Kate Seelye—for allowing me to present my research to a larger audience on January 19, 2011.

It is an enormous pleasure to work once again with the Johns Hopkins University Press, which published my first two books (*The Third World in Soviet Military Thought*, in 1982, and *Russia and*

Arabia: Soviet Foreign Policy toward the Arabian Peninsula, in 1986). I am especially grateful to the editor I worked with back then, Henry Tom, for encouraging me in early 2010 to undertake this project. It was a great shock to learn of his passing in early 2011. His death is an enormous loss not just to the Press but to all the many scholars whose work he helped to publish over the course of several decades. It has been wonderful, though, to work with my new JHU Press editor, Suzanne Flinchbaugh, who has been especially helpful in suggesting ways to reshape my draft into a book. Thanks are also due to Jeremy D. Horsefield (my copyeditor) and to everyone at the Press, especially those with whom I worked directly (Brendan Coyne, Kimberly Johnson, Juliana McCarthy, Martha Sewall, Claire Tamberino, and Karen Willmes), for all their fine work on this book.

I must also thank my old friend, Robert S. Litwak, Vice President for Programs and Director of International Security Studies at the Woodrow Wilson International Center for Scholars, and an anonymous reviewer for their comments and suggestions.

Thanks are also due to my wife, Nancy V. Yinger, and to my daughter, Melissa Y. Katz, for their advice, encouragement, and patience with me during all phases of this project. Finally, I would like to thank my mother, Eithne Dolores Dorney, for instilling in me an interest in international relations and encouraging me to pursue it. This book is dedicated to her.

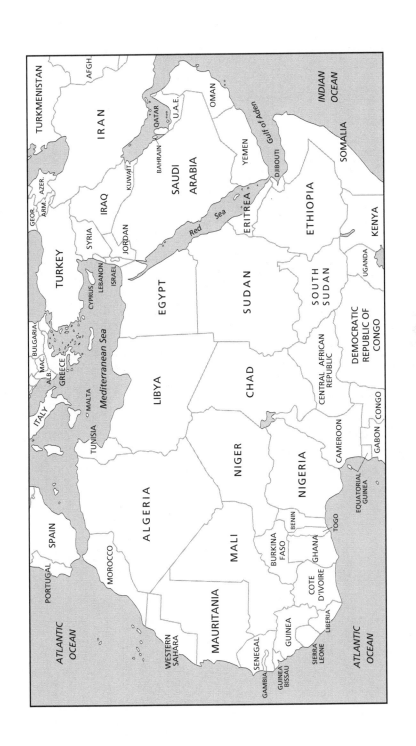

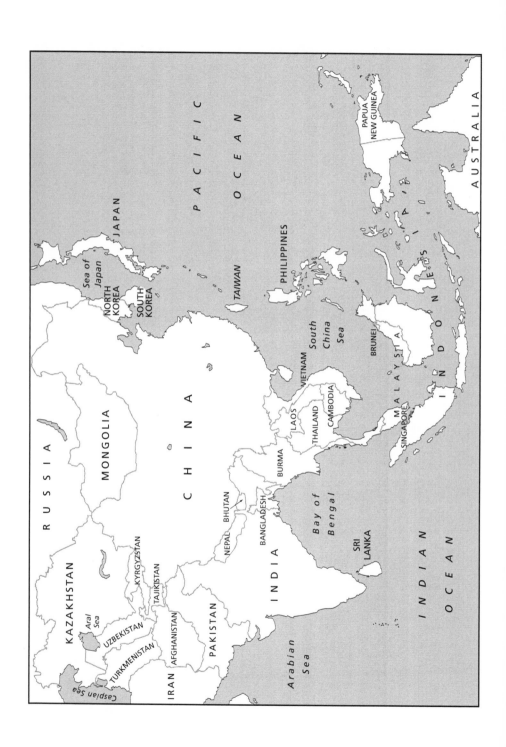

Leaving without Losing

▼ ▼ ▼

Prologue

The Beginning of the End
of the War on Terror?

On September 11, 2011, the War on Terror entered its second decade. Despite the death of Osama bin Laden on May 2, 2011, the War on Terror continues—with no end in sight.

Intervening in Afghanistan and Iraq has not led the United States to victory in the War on Terror. But withdrawing from these two countries will not either. The conflicts in them seem likely to continue—whether the United States stays or withdraws. Several other conflicts linked to the War on Terror—such as the Israeli-Palestinian conflict, the Indian-Pakistani dispute, and unrest in Yemen, Somalia, the North Caucasus, and elsewhere—also appear likely to persist indefinitely.

What should the United States do now? What can it do?

Although this volume does contain some suggestions as to what the United States ought to do, it is intended more to persuade Americans and their allies—whether proponents of the Bush approach, the Obama approach, or neither—to think differently about the War on Terror if they are to deal with it effectively. In this book, I argue the following: At the time of this writing, the United States has largely withdrawn from Iraq and is withdrawing from Afghanistan. This is reminiscent of the early

1970s when it withdrew from Indochina. Many negative consequences predicted by opponents of this earlier withdrawal did
indeed arise: the Marxists were emboldened with the knowledge
that the United States was unlikely to undertake another Vietnam. Similarly, Islamic radicals might now be emboldened by
the knowledge that the United States does not want another Iraq
or Afghanistan. But just as the U.S. withdrawal from Indochina
led to Marxist overconfidence and overexpansion in the 1970s
that the United States was then able to exploit, the U.S. withdrawal from Iraq and Afghanistan may similarly lead to Islamic
radical overconfidence and overexpansion that the United States
can also use to its advantage. Withdrawal, in other words, need
not mean defeat.

In addition, the War on Terror resembles the Cold War (especially in the Third World) in that it is not just one conflict but
includes numerous regional and local conflicts that are linked,
but which have their own separate dynamics. The United States
could reduce the intensity of the War on Terror if it could resolve
some of these conflicts and thus decouple them from it. But as
the U.S. experience during the Cold War showed, this is not easy
to accomplish.

The United States must also be mindful not only of how new
factors—such as the Arab Spring—affect the War on Terror but
of how the War on Terror fits into the larger geopolitical context. Ironically, while American overextension in Afghanistan and
Iraq may have assisted the efforts of other countries to further
their own great power ambitions, U.S. withdrawals may actually
affect some of them more negatively than they do the United
States.

Finally, while the War on Terror now appears to be endless, so
did the Cold War to those who lived through it. The Cold War
did, however, come to an end. The War on Terror can too.

The War on Terror in Perspective

▼ ▼ ▼

The Second Decade of the War on Terror

One prediction about the War on Terror can be made with great confidence: it is not going to end any time soon. There are several directions, though, in which it could evolve. The likelihood of four scenarios concerning its future direction are examined here (from the viewpoint of America and many of its allies): an implausible best case, an implausible worst case, a plausible good case, and a plausible bad case.

Implausible Best Case: Holding the Jihadists at Bay

From the American viewpoint, the best-case scenario for the War on Terror—short of its miraculously ending or dramatically subsiding—is that radical Islamists make no further significant political gains despite American withdrawal and despite a basically unaltered American foreign policy (for example, the United States continues to support Israel and numerous authoritarian governments in the Muslim world). For even if jihadists (self-defined Islamic holy warriors) cannot be eliminated or prevented from launching terrorist attacks on civilian targets in the West and in the Muslim world, it would be an important accomplishment just to prevent them from overthrowing governments allied to the United States or to significantly weaken them. And if they could be held at bay for long enough, the jihadists' aura of success—as well as support for them—might be greatly diminished. Jihadi efforts might then be successfully undermined (even if slowly) through a combination of intelligent police work, taking advantage of internal rifts to co-opt some of them, and economic and political reforms that provide better opportunities than what the jihadists offer for ordinary citizens to achieve their aspirations.

This is not an unattractive scenario, but it does not appear to be a realistic one. So long as authoritarian governments generate internal opposition (which they usually do), and so long as American support for these regimes generates resentment against the United States (which it often does), removing U.S. influence from their respective countries is likely to be seen as a necessary condition for removing the unpopular authoritarian regimes that Washington supports.

Not all authoritarian regimes in the Muslim world, of course, are destined to be overthrown by radical Islamist movements as was the U.S.-backed Shah of Iran in that country's 1979 revolution. Indeed, authoritarian regimes in the Muslim world—whether backed by the United States or not—have been remarkably good (up until 2011) at staying in power since the 1970s or even before. But is it reasonable to expect that no other pro-Western regime, or even anti-Western but secular authoritarian regime, in the Muslim world—of which there are many—will not be replaced by a radical Islamist one? Such an expectation does not seem reasonable, especially since revolution can occur not only by means of a slow-moving insurgency, which may (or may not) be stopped, but also by way of a rapid, unexpected popular uprising (as occurred in Tunisia and Egypt in 2011) or through a coup d'état. Such movements can lead to democratization, but they can also lead to radical Islamic revolution.

It seems far more reasonable to expect, then, that more Islamic revolutionary regimes are going to arise as the War on Terror continues.

Implausible Worst Case: The Rise of a Hostile Caliphate

Believing that it was primarily the resistance effort of the mujahideen that brought about not only the Soviet withdrawal from Afghanistan but also the collapse of communism and the downfall of the Soviet Union, Osama bin Laden optimistically predicted prior to 9/11 that the jihadists could also force the United States out of the Muslim world. Indeed, he suggested that defeating the United States would be easier than defeating the USSR since Americans were far more averse to casualties than the Soviets were. Bin Laden cited the withdrawal of American forces from Lebanon in 1984 and from Somalia in 1994 after spectacular attacks against them as proof of this proposition. Furthermore, he reasoned, once the United States had withdrawn from the Muslim world, the governments it supported there would fall, and the caliphate uniting the entire Muslim world would arise (Cole 2004).

Bin Laden may have anticipated, then, that the 9/11 attacks would result in the American withdrawal from the Muslim world that he had predicted and hoped for. But if this was his expectation, he clearly miscalculated. Far from leaving the Muslim world, the Bush administration launched military interventions first in Afghanistan (which forced bin Laden into hiding across the border in Pakistan) and then in Iraq. This increased American involvement in these two Muslim countries, plus the greater American presence in the Muslim world generally following 9/11, meant that the second and third parts of bin Laden's prediction—that following the American departure from the Muslim world, the governments it supported would fall and the caliphate would arise—did not come true either.

As of this writing, however, the United States has largely withdrawn from Iraq and has begun withdrawing from Afghanistan. It seems unlikely that the United States will be willing to engage in additional major military interventions in the Muslim world any time soon, especially since the U.S./NATO action begun in 2011 against Libya did not succeed in ousting Qaddafi as quickly or painlessly as was hoped. Does this mean that bin Laden's prediction now has a greater chance of realization? Was he just a decade off on its timing? For if the U.S. withdrawal leads to the downfall of some U.S.-backed governments in the Muslim world (much as the U.S. withdrawal from Indochina in 1973 was followed by the downfall of governments allied to the United States in South Vietnam, Laos, and Cambodia in 1975), and if any new radical Islamist governments were to arise and unite into a "caliphate" that threatens to absorb even more countries, this certainly would be the worst case for America and its allies.

But just as the best-case scenario outlined above appears unrealistic, this worst-case one does too—for three reasons. First, American withdrawals from Iraq and Afghanistan are not likely to lead to a U.S. departure from the Muslim world as a whole. While American domestic politics in the wake of the long, frustrating conflicts in these two countries, plus another one in Libya, may reduce U.S. willingness to directly intervene elsewhere, this does not mean that it will stop supplying arms and other assistance to allied governments in the region fighting against radical Islamist forces.

Second, even in the unlikely case that America did withdraw from the Muslim world, bin Laden's assumption that the governments it had been supporting would then fall is questionable. Some may well be able to remain in power either with assistance from other countries or with their own resources. While it is unrealistic to expect that all existing governments in the Muslim world will be able to resist radical Islamist forces following the U.S. withdrawal from Iraq and Afghanistan, it is also unrealistic to expect that all—or even many—of them will succumb to them. And as the cases of Tunisia and Egypt in early 2011 showed, long-ruling authoritarian leaders may be overthrown not by radical Islamists but by democratic revolutions (or at least aspiring ones) instead.

Finally, even if a few (or many) radical Islamist regimes do come to power, it is highly unlikely that they are going to merge into a larger, single state, or would remain united for long. Someone possessing the skill, determination, ruthlessness, and overweening ego that it takes to overthrow an existing regime and set up his own is simply not the type of person who will then, for purely ideological reasons, surrender control over his country to someone similar in another country. Such a person is far more likely to insist on maintaining control and will find or invent whatever ideological justification is necessary to do so. Such a person is also far more likely to convince himself that he should be acknowledged as the leader of the transnational Islamist revolutionary movement and that nobody else is as deserving. As with the Marxist-Leninist and Arab nationalist revolutionary waves that splintered and failed earlier, the spread of the radical Islamic revolutionary wave to more countries is less likely to lead to unity than to rifts and rivalries among them.

Plausible Good Case: Withdrawal Goes Well

It is widely anticipated that after the United States withdraws from Iraq and Afghanistan, events will take a turn for the worse in these two countries. Iraq may descend into civil war or fall under Iranian influence. The Taliban may return to power in Afghanistan. The enormous sacrifices made by America and its allies will have been made for nothing.

These predictions are partially based on the historical experience of what happened after America and other countries ended long, unsuccessful counterinsurgency efforts elsewhere. For instance, the withdrawal of American forces in early 1973, after fighting in Indochina for nearly a decade without being able to defeat the Marxist insurgencies there, was soon followed by communist takeovers in South Vietnam, Laos, and Cambodia in 1975. Similarly, following the withdrawal of Soviet forces from Afghanistan in 1989 after nearly a decade of fighting, the Marxist regime that Moscow had been defending fell to mujahideen forces in 1992. There are many other similar examples.

But this is not always what happens. The end of Egypt's long-drawn-out counterinsurgency effort in North Yemen in the 1960s was quite different from the outcome America experienced in Indochina or the Soviet Union experienced in Afghanistan. President Nasser sent tens of thousands of Egyptian troops to bolster the fledgling Yemen Arab Republic that came into being on September 26, 1962, when the newly installed monarch of this country was overthrown by his military. The king, however, was able to flee the capital, rally the northern tribes, and obtain aid from Saudi Arabia. Instead of the simple victory that Nasser hoped for, he found himself bogged down in a long-drawn-out war in which Egypt (which had far more troops in the country than the North Yemeni republic they were defending) was unable to overcome the Saudi-backed royalists.

After the humiliating defeat at the hands of Israel that Egypt, Jordan, and Syria suffered in the 1967 Arab-Israeli War, Nasser sought improved relations with Saudi Arabia and agreed to withdraw all Egyptian forces from North Yemen forthwith. It was widely believed at the time that the North Yemeni republic would soon fall, especially when royalists completely surrounded the capital, Sana'a. But the Yemen Arab Republic, as was previously noted, did not fall. Benefiting from a brief but vital Soviet airlift of supplies, as well as dissension within the ranks of the royalists, the republic survived. The war finally came to an end in 1970 with the help of a Saudi-mediated settlement allowing the royalists (minus the royal family) to become integrated into the republic.

North Yemen is not the only example of something like this happening. For instance, at the end of the Cold War, Cuban forces withdrew from Angola, where they had been aiding the Marxist regime against a white South African–backed insurgency, and Vietnamese forces withdrew from Cambodia, where they had been aiding the pro-Hanoi regime they had installed in 1978 when they ousted the anti-Hanoi (and Chinese-backed) Khmer Rouge, who sought a return to power. In both cases these beleaguered governments survived and remained in power (albeit after years of more fighting in Angola and UN intervention in Cambodia).

Could something like this happen in either Iraq or Afghanistan? If American and other coalition forces were to leave, their withdrawal may actually serve to enhance the legitimacy of the Iraqi and Afghan governments and give them the opportunity to deal with their opponents in their own manner instead of having their actions constantly second-guessed and micromanaged by

Washington officials. Further, just as their opponents have been able to make use of the large American presence to label the Iraqi and Afghan governments as acting on behalf of the United States, the absence of American forces might well afford these governments the opportunity to label their opponents as acting on behalf of Pakistan in the case of Afghanistan and on behalf of Iran or its other neighbors in the case of Iraq.

It is also possible that these two countries might actually become prosperous. In a *Wall Street Journal* op-ed piece published December 21, 2010, Bartle Bull (the founder of an Iraq-focused investment bank) predicted that Iraq will surpass Saudi Arabia as the world's largest oil exporter and may experience "one of the largest economic reconstruction and development booms in history." The enormous mineral wealth possessed by Afghanistan—which came to light in 2010—gives that country the *potential* for its own development boom (Risen 2010). Forecasts such as these, of course, will appear naively optimistic to many, including within these two countries. But very few predicted in 1975 that both China and Vietnam would experience strong economic growth, would establish strong trade relations with the West, *and* would still be ruled by their authoritarian communist regimes.

It is by no means foreordained that things will go as well in Iraq and Afghanistan following American withdrawals as has been outlined here. But as the experience of other countries suggests, when foreign forces withdraw from a country they had been occupying or supporting, those regimes do not necessarily fall. Similarly, countries impoverished by war and revolution can still go on to become prosperous.

Plausible Bad Case: A Multitude of Conflicts

While they are (as discussed earlier) unlikely to unite in a caliphate, a number of other negative consequences are likely to emerge along with any new radical Islamist regimes. First, and most obviously, since many predominantly Muslim states also happen to be major petroleum producers, radical Islamic revolutions that occur in these particular states or neighboring ones will lead to disruptions in petroleum supplies to the world market, or to fears that these will occur. Either of these can lead to spikes in petroleum prices that negatively affect petroleum-importing countries.

As Stephen M. Walt observed in his book *Revolution and War* (1996), revolution in one country very often leads to war between it and others. And even when war does not result from revolution, tensions between new revolutionary regimes and neighboring states tend to increase. More Islamic revolutionary regimes coming into being, then, are likely to result in more wars and tensions between them and neighboring states. And states that suddenly find themselves to be the neighbors of these new, unwelcome revolutionary regimes are likely to call upon America and others for protection. These new revolutionary regimes may call upon others for protection too. And if this unfolds alongside a heightened competition among existing and aspiring great powers worldwide, their rivalries may become enmeshed in these local rivalries between revolutionary and nonrevolutionary states.

The most important consequence of additional radical Islamist regimes coming to power, though, may be the intensification of and increase in internal conflicts in countries where they do. As argued later in this book, a significant obstacle to President George W. Bush's ambitious plans for the democratization of the greater Middle East is the legacy of history resulting in the rule of ethnic or sectarian minorities in many states and/or the desire of ethnically distinct regions within them to secede. This legacy of history poses difficulties not only for democratization but also for radical Islamist regimes. One of the aspirations of Islamist ideology is to try to overcome existing ethnic (if not sectarian) conflicts in predominantly Muslim countries by establishing Islamic identity as primary. The problem with radical Islamist (as well as other authoritarian) regimes is that they tend not to be inclusive, but to be (or become) dominated by a specific group. The Islamic Republic of Iran, for example, is ruled mainly by Shi'a Persians, not by non-Persians and especially not by non-Shi'as. The Islamist regime that has ruled Sudan since 1989 has been dominated by Sunni Arabs, not by non-Muslims (such as those in the South) or non-Arab Muslims (such as those in Darfur). The Taliban in Afghanistan is a predominantly Pushtun movement that holds little appeal for non-Pushtuns.

Should radical Islamist regimes come to power elsewhere, it is doubtful that they will rule in a more tolerant and less authoritarian manner than the Iranian, Sudanese, or Afghan Taliban regimes have done. While they may come to power hoping to spread their revolution to other countries, their more lasting effect may be the initiation or intensification of internal conflicts within their own country that either threaten or result in its breakup. Sudan is a case in point. The radical Islamic regime that came to power there in 1989 earnestly set about attempting to export its brand of revolution to neighboring countries. Not only did it fail at this, but its efforts to impose strict Islamic rule on non-Muslim southern Sudan resulted in a fierce war that has in turn resulted in the independence of South Sudan and a secessionist movement in Darfur. This may also be the fate of other countries where radical Islamist regimes come to power.

While the worst case of a united radical Islamist caliphate emerging is highly implausible, this pessimistic scenario of more Islamic revolutions leading to more conflicts within and between states seems all too plausible. Many conflicts involving small countries will not pose the same existential threat to the rest of the world that a hostile caliphate stretching from Morocco to Indonesia would. On the other hand, managing the many conflicts that this plausible pessimistic scenario envisages will not be easy. Even worse, the resolution of any one conflict may have little impact on the many others not linked to it.

What Should America Do Now?

It is not yet clear which of the cases outlined here most accurately predicts the future of the War on Terror, or whether it will take a direction not yet envisioned. Indeed, the actual scenario may be a mixed one: going well (from the Western and moderate Muslim viewpoint) in some places, not so well in others, and absolutely horrifically in others still. What does seem certain, however, is that the War on Terror will continue for years or even decades to come.

As the War on Terror enters its second decade, there do not appear to be any easy options for the United States to bring this set of conflicts to an end or to extricate itself from them. What is needed now are new ways to think about four specific questions that, in my view, need to be understood in order to develop intelligent and sensible policies going forward.

Understanding What Went Wrong in the First Decade. President George W. Bush's approach toward the War on Terror is now generally seen as unsuccessful. But understanding why it was unsuccessful is crucial for understanding whether President Barack Obama's changed approach to it can achieve more satisfactory results.

Opportunities after Withdrawal. The Obama administration's decision to withdraw American forces from these two countries is unlikely to be reversed. But while withdrawal clearly poses risks, it may also present opportunities that Washington can take advantage of, provided that it is aware of them.

Beyond Iraq and Afghanistan. There are many other conflicts and problems linked to the War on Terror, several of which long predate it. Some of them might be decoupled from the War on Terror, but only if Washington approaches them differently than it has up to now.

New Factors and Broader Contexts. What is the effect of new factors such as the death of Osama bin Laden and (more importantly) the Arab uprisings that began in 2011? How does the War on Terror fit into the broader geopolitical and historical contexts?

Before addressing these questions, something first needs to be said about just what the War on Terror is.

▼ ▼ ▼

What Exactly Is the War on Terror?

The phrase "War on Terror" was popularized by President George W. Bush and his administration in the aftermath of 9/11. It has been widely criticized ever since. Terror, after all, is a tactic. How, many asked, can war be waged against a tactic? Others claimed (rightly or wrongly) that many U.S. allies—or even the United States itself—also engaged in terror, or "state terrorism." "Terrorists," then, was what the U.S. government called those whom it dislikes, but not those whom it does like—even if (the argument runs) they engage in similar activities. In addition, many have claimed that the "War on Terror" is really a war against certain Muslim actors that Washington dislikes, or even against Islam itself.

The U.S. government argues that it is not at war with Islam or Muslims in general, but only with radical Islamists who engage in terrorism. In March 2009, Secretary of State Hillary Clinton announced that the Obama administration had stopped using the Bush-era War on Terror terminology (Solomon 2009). But coming up with an alternative phrase has proven difficult. The Obama administration reportedly tried to replace it with the phrase "Overseas Contingency Operation" (Wilson and Kamen

2009) but quickly dropped this. More recently, it has begun referring to its efforts as "Countering Violent Extremism," or CVE (Johnson 2010). Even the Bush administration used other terms, including the "Global War on Terror" (or GWOT) and the "Long War." Bush's first defense secretary, Donald Rumsfeld, reportedly promoted the term "Global Struggle against Violent Extremism" (or GSAVE), but Bush himself rejected this (Wilson and Kamen 2009). Indeed, it seems that all the alternatives to the phrase "the War on Terror" are rather awkward and have simply not caught on. Despite its flaws, the War on Terror remains the term whereby the ongoing struggle between the United States and its allies on the one hand and Al Qaeda and other radical Islamist movements and governments on the other is popularly known. And so this term will be employed here.

The War on Terror is not the first imprecise phrase that has become the popularly accepted term for a global conflict. The Cold War was another. The term Cold War was intended to differentiate the Soviet-American conflict from a "hot war" that involved actual armed conflict between great powers, as in World Wars I and II. But in many parts of the world, there was nothing cold about the Cold War. Asia, the Middle East, Africa, and Latin America experienced many actual wars, with the United States and the USSR actively supporting opposing sides in them. Further, American armed forces became heavily involved in multiyear wars in Korea and Indochina while Soviet armed forces fought a long war in Afghanistan. Yet despite its inaccuracy, the Cold War was the term that was—and still is—used to designate the era between 1945 and 1991 when Soviet-American competition was the predominant feature of international relations. Similarly, the War on Terror is the common designation for the era since September 11, 2001, when the ongoing struggle between the United States and its allies on the one hand and Al Qaeda and other radical Islamist movements and governments on the other became the predominant feature of international relations.

Besides being the commonly accepted designations for different eras, the Cold War and the War on Terror have something else in common: the eras they designate refer to not just one conflict but many conflicts that, to a greater or lesser extent, were or are linked to one another. While Soviet-American competition was the predominant feature of the Cold War, many other conflicts occurred in different regions of the world during this era. These conflicts had their own distinct issues and causes—such as the quest for independence from European colonial rule, ethnoreligious rivalry, border disputes, secessionist attempts, and others. In addition to the local actors and issues involved, competition between Moscow and Washington was so pervasive and widespread that most (if not all) conflicts occurring during the Cold War era also had a Soviet-American dimension. Indeed, this Soviet-American dimension was often seen (whether correctly or incorrectly) as more important than the local dimensions of various regional conflicts—and even as the primary cause of such conflicts.

Similarly, while the U.S. government and Al Qaeda and many of its affiliates see themselves as engaged in an all-pervasive, worldwide struggle, the War on Terror era includes many other conflicts in which the U.S. versus Al Qaeda element is present, but which also have their own distinct dimensions. A short list includes conflicts in Iraq, Afghanistan, Yemen, and Somalia, as well as those between Israel and the Palestinians, India and Pakistan, and many others. Indeed, although the Cold War ended some two decades ago, some of the regional conflicts that were part of it continued and have become part of the War on Terror. These include the Israeli-Palestinian, Indian-Pakistani, and Afghan conflicts.

There is, however, an important difference between these two eras: while the Cold War ended some two decades ago, the War on Terror has not ended, and it does not appear likely to any time soon. The fact that the prolonged Cold War finally ended raises the possibility that the War on Terror can also be brought to a conclusion. The Cold War that began in 1945 lasted some forty-six years, while the Soviet revolutionary regime that arose during the 1917 Russian Revolution remained in power for over seventy-four years. If dated from 9/11, the War on Terror has only been in existence for just over a decade. Of course, Al Qaeda's struggle against the United States began earlier—at the time of the 1990–91 Kuwait crisis. The U.S. conflict with radical Islam began even earlier still, with the 1979 Iranian Revolution—just as the Russian conflict with radical Islam began with the 1979 Soviet invasion of Afghanistan. Yet even if this earlier date is chosen, the Western (and Russian) struggle against Islamic radicalism has only lasted just over three decades so far. If the longevity of the Cold War or the Soviet Union is a guide as to how long the War on Terror might last, it may still have many years or even decades to run. Worse still, the continuation of several regional conflicts that took place during the Cold War long after its demise raises the possibility that even if the War on Terror does somehow come to an end, many (if not all) of the current regional and local component conflicts may well grind on afterward.

UNDERSTANDING WHAT WENT WRONG
IN THE FIRST DECADE

▼ ▼ ▼

Assessing the Bush Strategy

If someone else had been president of the United States instead of George W. Bush at the time of the 9/11 attacks (such as Al Gore—the winner of the popular but not the Electoral College vote in 2000), would he also have invaded Afghanistan and Iraq? Was it a good idea for the United States to invade Afghanistan and Iraq instead of pursuing other policies in response both to 9/11 and to whatever challenge Saddam Hussein posed? Although these are interesting questions that can be—indeed, have been—debated at length, they are essentially irrelevant. George W. Bush was president when 9/11 occurred, and it was his administration that conceptualized the War on Terror and designed a strategy for prosecuting it that included the U.S.-led invasions of Afghanistan and Iraq in 2001 and 2003, respectively.

The more relevant question to ask about Bush's War on Terror policies is, to what extent were they successful? Bush's War on Terror, of course, did not just have one goal, but several. One of Bush's announced goals was to prevent another 9/11 type of attack on American soil, and at this he succeeded: there was no similar attack on U.S. soil either during the remainder of his presidency or afterward. This does not mean, of course, that it couldn't happen again. And Al Qaeda (or its sympathizers) have launched deadly attacks in many countries allied to the United States, including Britain, Spain, Indonesia, and others. Still, the fear that arose at the time of 9/11 that it might be just the beginning of a series of major attacks inside the United States has not been borne out.

Another of Bush's stated goals was that U.S. forces would capture or kill Osama bin Laden and destroy Al Qaeda. While Bush did not achieve either of these two goals, his successor—Barack Obama—did achieve the first of these when bin Laden was killed in 2011. Still, bin Laden's deputy, Ayman al-Zawahiri, and other Al Qaeda leaders remain at large. More importantly, Al Qaeda's many affiliates—if not Al Qaeda itself—have increased their activity in many countries in the Muslim world and elsewhere.

The two signature policies of Bush's War on Terror—the invasions of Afghanistan and Iraq—have had mixed results. On the one hand, the two invasions succeeded in driving out of power the Taliban and the Saddam Hussein regimes—both of which were highly authoritarian, repressive, and hostile toward the United States. On the other hand, the United States has not succeeded in establishing peace and security in either country even after many years of fighting.

There was yet another highly ambitious goal that President Bush announced: the democratization of the greater Middle East. In his speech of November 6, 2003, marking the twentieth anniversary of the National Endowment for Democracy (NED), Bush stated,

> Sixty years of Western nations excusing and accommodating the lack of freedom in the Middle East did nothing to make us safe—because in the long run, stability cannot be purchased at the expense of liberty. As long as the Middle East remains a place where freedom does not flourish, it will remain a place of stagnation, resentment, and violence ready for export. And with the spread of weapons that can bring catastrophic harm to our country and to our friends, it would be reckless to accept the status quo.

Therefore, the United States has adopted a new policy, a forward strategy of freedom in the Middle East. This strategy requires the same persistence and energy and idealism we have shown before. And it will yield the same results. As in Europe, as in Asia, as in every region of the world, the advance of freedom leads to peace.

Bush, then, sought the democratization not only of the two countries that the United States had invaded but of the greater Middle East generally. In this speech, Bush also pointed to progress toward democratization in Morocco, Bahrain, Oman, Qatar, Yemen, Kuwait, Jordan, and even Saudi Arabia. In addition, he called upon Palestinian, Iranian, and Egyptian leaders to move forward along the path of democratization.

Clearly, President Bush did not achieve this ambitious goal. The United States has fostered democracy in Iraq, but it is extremely fragile and has not succeeded in overcoming Iraq's bitter ethnic and sectarian divisions. There is strong reason to doubt whether Iraqi democracy will survive the withdrawal of American armed forces. Afghanistan appears to be a democracy in name only, despite the continued presence of American and NATO forces. Further, Bush's hopes for progress toward democratization in all the other Middle Eastern countries he mentioned were not fulfilled. (In 2011, hope for democratization arose in Egypt, but this was not due to its American-allied leader, Hosni Mubarak, moving forward along this path, but to his being deposed instead.) Although Pakistan may have become more democratic, it certainly does not appear to have become more peaceful or willing to cooperate with the United States with regard to the Taliban and Al Qaeda.

What was remarkable about Bush's NED speech was that it was a repudiation of previous American foreign policy toward the Middle East. He essentially blamed American support for dictatorial regimes as causing the "stagnation, resentment, and violence ready for export" that allowed Al Qaeda and similar groups to thrive. American support for democratization in the greater Middle East, by contrast, would lead to peace and prosperity there as it had elsewhere. If given the opportunity to pursue their political and economic ambitions through democratic means, Bush seemed to expect, most Arabs and Muslims would not support authoritarian opposition movements such as Al Qaeda.

While Bush's desire to see democracy spread throughout the Middle East was criticized by many as ill-advised and impractical, it was noteworthy that Bush thought not only that the United States should do this but also that it could do so successfully. He rejected the notion that there were unique religious and cultural barriers to democratization in the Middle East.

So why, then, didn't his efforts succeed? Some might argue that, despite Bush's claims, there actually are unique religious and cultural barriers to democratization in the Middle East. Islam and democracy, the argument runs, are simply incompatible. This argument, however, is belied by the fact that democracy is being successfully practiced in several predominantly Muslim countries. The democracy watchdog organization Freedom House designated several predominantly Muslim countries as electoral democracies in 2011, including Albania, Bangladesh, Bosnia-Herzegovina, Indonesia, Maldives, Mali, and Turkey (Freedom House 2011). Despite repression against them, strong democratic opposition movements arose in Iran in 2009 and in several Arab countries in 2011. Finally, many Muslims in predominantly non-Muslim countries—including the United States, United Kingdom, India, and many more—have become active and successful participants in their democratic processes. In light of this, other, more satisfactory explanations for the Middle East's lack of progress toward democratization need to be considered.

Two readily come to mind. First and foremost, the Middle East's many authoritarian regimes do not want to embark on democratization since this would no doubt lead to their fall from power. Both pro-American and anti-American authoritarian regimes are agreed on this point. Second, after Hamas won the Palestinian parliamentary elections of 2006 and refused to change its hard-line position on Israel, the Bush administration de-emphasized its democratization efforts in much of the region. Free elections, it seemed to realize, would not necessarily result in the victory of pro-American parties either in the Occupied

Territories or elsewhere in the greater Middle East. Despite its policy differences with the Bush administration, the Obama administration appeared to have adopted a similar attitude—at least until the outbreak of democratic revolution in the Arab world in 2011.

How can the disappointing progress toward democracy in both Iraq and Afghanistan be explained? Unlike other countries in the greater Middle East, the United States—along with several of its allies—has occupied these two countries for several years at enormous cost. While the United States had little real opportunity and did not try particularly hard to promote democracy elsewhere in the region, it has had plenty of opportunity and has tried very hard to do so in these two countries. Why the United States has met with only fragile—possibly ephemeral—success fostering democracy in Iraq and has largely failed to do so in Afghanistan requires a closer look at each of these two countries.

▼ ▼ ▼

══════════════
══════════════
══════════════

Why Couldn't the United States
Foster Democracy in Iraq?

Although the United States intervened in Iraq after it began its intervention in Afghanistan, it began withdrawing from Iraq before doing so from Afghanistan. Therefore, what the United States has and has not accomplished in Iraq will be discussed first.

While the United States created the conditions that have allowed Iraq to hold national and local elections, it has not been able to persuade or cajole important Iraqi groups to fully—or even less than fully—cooperate with one another. The Arab Shi'a–Arab Sunni rivalry is especially important. There are also differences within the Arab Shi'a community, and Arab-Kurdish divisions remain. Certainly the inability of a government to be formed for over nine months after the March 7, 2010, parliamentary elections did not bode well for the prospects for democracy and stability in Iraq.

The United States certainly bears some responsibility for Iraq's failure to make a smooth transition to democracy. The Bush administration could have sent more troops to keep order in Iraq after the downfall of Saddam and planned more carefully for the transition afterward. The United States also could have done much more to prevent and halt the ethnic cleansing campaigns that took place. And if America had done these things, it may have been easier for Iraqi politicians from different communities (as well as political parties) to work together cooperatively.

The United States, however, is not responsible for the hostility that exists among Iraq's three main communities. This is something that predated the U.S.-led intervention that began in 2003. As is well known, Saddam Hussein's regime was based on and privileged the Arab Sunni minority, which dominated the Arab Shi'a majority, the Kurdish minority, and Iraq's many other smaller communities. What is less well known (at least in the West) is that Arab Sunni minority dominance did not begin with Saddam Hussein but long predated him. As Hanna Batatu wrote about in his magisterial book, *The Old Social Classes and the Revolutionary Movements of Iraq* (1978), the Ottoman Turks who ruled Iraq through the end of World War I, the British who took their place, and the British-installed Hashemite monarchy that presided until its overthrow in 1958 all relied on Arab Sunnis to maintain their rule over Iraq's other communities. The "Free Officers" who overthrew the monarchy in 1958 were also predominantly Arab Sunni.

Before it came to power, the Iraqi Ba'th Party primarily attracted members from that country's dispossessed Arab Shi'a and other communities. But as the Ba'th succeeded in recruiting Iraqi army officers, its military wing came to be increasingly dominated by Arab Sunnis. Between the downfall of the first Ba'th regime (which only held power for a few months in 1963) and the rise to power of the second Ba'th regime in 1968, a sectarian power struggle (in which Saddam Hussein played a leading role) occurred within the party's ranks that resulted in the triumph of the predominantly Arab Sunni military wing. His regime, then, did not change but reinforced the existing pattern of Arab Sunni dominance over Arab Shi'as, Kurds, and others.

With the American-led invasion and subsequent elections, the United States ended the Arab Sunni dominance over Iraq's other communities, as well as over Iraq, that had been in existence since the Ottoman era. The subsequent American occupation allowed the Kurds to solidify their rule over northern Iraq and parties representing the Arab Shi'a majority to gain control of the parliament. Deeply resenting these outcomes, it is not surprising that initially Arab Sunnis fiercely resisted the American occupation. Fueling this resistance was the firmly held belief of many Arab Sunnis that they were not a minority but the majority in Iraq. And whether they had benefited from or suffered under Saddam's rule, Arab Sunnis came to fear—often with good reason—how they would be treated by the resentful Arab Shi'as empowered by the American intervention. Since Saddam's regime was dominated by Arab Sunnis, the disbanding of Saddam's armed forces and the de-Ba'thification campaign undertaken by the American occupation authorities most strongly affected Arab Sunnis (and most especially elite Arab Sunnis). The Arab Shi'a–dominated Iraqi government's continued pursuit of former Ba'thists is seen by many Arab Sunnis as an effort to exclude them from the political process (Moaddel, Tessler, and Inglehart 2008–9).

The Arab Shi'a majority, of course, is pleased that the American-led intervention has resulted in its finally coming to power. This does not mean, however, that the Arab Shi'as (or factions within this community) approved the continuation of the American occupation. Having been dominated so long by the Arab Sunnis, the Arab Shi'as very much fear a reversion to this situation. While the U.S. military congratulated itself on having turned many of the previously hostile Arab Sunni tribes into allies fighting alongside it, many Arab Shi'as saw this, as well as American efforts to integrate Arab Sunnis into the Iraqi armed forces, as presaging the return of Arab Sunni dominance over them. During both the Ottoman and British periods, cooperation with external forces was what allowed Arab Sunnis to dominate other communities in Iraq. Arab Shi'a politicians feared that Arab Sunni cooperation with the Americans could lead to a similar result, and so they resisted American efforts to integrate Arab Sunnis into the new Arab Shi'a–dominated Iraqi security forces.

American intervention also altered the Kurdish dimension of Iraqi politics. Kurdish aspirations for independence have been frustrated not only by the Arab Sunnis of Iraq but also by Turkey and Iran (where large numbers of Kurds also live in regions bordering northern Iraq) and by internecine conflict among the Kurds themselves, which others have exploited. The Kurds were able to take advantage of American hostility toward Saddam Hussein to create their own autonomous zone in northern Iraq after the 1990–91 Kuwait conflict and to solidify their rule over this region after the 2003 American-led intervention. Although the Kurdish region is nominally still part of Iraq, Baghdad does not exercise authority over it. Kurdish politicians do, however, play an important political role in Baghdad through both controlling a key bloc in the parliament and holding important offices such as president and foreign minister.

The U.S.-led intervention and efforts to promote democratization, then, completely upended relations among Iraq's three principle communities. American actions ended Arab Sunni domination over both the Arab Shi'a majority and the Kurdish minority and created a situation in which the Arab Shi'a majority dominates the national government, the Kurdish minority dominates its homeland in northern Iraq, and even the Arab Sunni minority holds sway in its tribal heartland in western Iraq. As was mentioned earlier, the United States did succeed in holding and protecting relatively free and fair elections in Iraq. Unfortunately, it did not succeed in establishing genuine reconciliation among Iraq's three main communities. And if national reconciliation did not occur when America maintained a large military presence in Iraq, it does not appear likely that this will occur after the end of the American military presence.

The future of Iraq and the balance of power among its three main communities is not clear at present and may not be for a long time. Although the United States ended Arab Sunni minority dominance over the country, it was unable to establish peace among Iraq's three main communities, which suggests that stable democracy will have difficulty taking root in Iraq.

▼ ▼ ▼

Why Couldn't the United States
Foster Democracy in Afghanistan?

At this point, the prospects for building a stable democracy in Afghanistan appear nonexistent, whether or not American forces remain there. American policy must bear much of the blame for this state of affairs. Had the United States not intervened in Iraq and devoted the resources that it lavished on that conflict and used them instead in Afghanistan, perhaps the security situation there could have been stabilized and the prospects for democratization would have been better. But even if intervention in Iraq had not occurred, the American-led democratization effort in Afghanistan was flawed from the beginning. Unlike in Iraq, where the United States constructed a parliamentary system with some checks and balances and which had both local and national elections, the system the U.S. government set up in Afghanistan is a centralized presidential system with a weak parliament unable to check the president, who also appoints all the provincial governors. Further, rather than overseeing a process allowing Afghans to freely choose their first post-Taliban president, the Bush administration selected Hamid Karzai for this position and pushed the Afghans into ratifying this choice.

To be fair, one of the Bush administration's motives for choosing Karzai was that it hoped that he would be able to overcome Afghanistan's ethnic divides and enjoy national support. A Pushtun from southern Afghanistan, Karzai was reputed to have strong connections in the non-Pushtun north. Thus, in addition to being able to work well with northerners, it was hoped that Karzai would appeal to his fellow Pushtuns and draw them away from the Taliban. This, unfortunately, has not occurred. In addition to being seen as corrupt, ineffective, and having fraudulently won reelection in 2009, Karzai does not appear to have strong support in either the north or the south of the country.

There are other obstacles to democracy and stability in Afghanistan, however, for which the United States is not responsible. Foremost among these is neighboring Pakistan's inability—indeed, unwillingness—to stop the Afghan Taliban from making use of safe haven in Pakistani territory bordering Afghanistan or from supporting their colleagues across the border in frustrating Western nation-building efforts. Pakistan has pursued an ambiguous policy of supporting both the U.S./NATO military mission in Afghanistan and the Taliban. Pakistan backed the Taliban during its rise to power in the mid-1990s and during 1996–2001, when the Taliban ruled most of the country. Powerful elements within the Pakistani military and intelligence establishment reportedly perceived this as advantageous to Pakistan in relation to its ongoing competition with India. And so Islamabad continued to support the Afghan Taliban as an ally opposing the rise of Indian influence in Afghanistan (Pape and Feldman 2010, 117–19). Washington, for its part, has so far been unable to persuade Pakistan—which provides transit routes for American military supplies to Afghanistan—to end its support for the Taliban. Pakistan, then, has facilitated the resurgence of the Taliban.

The United States is also not responsible for the hostility that exists between Afghanistan's ethnic communities—especially between the Pushtuns in the south and the non-Pushtuns (Uzbeks, Tajiks, Hazaras, and others) elsewhere. As in Iraq, this is something that long predated the U.S.-led intervention after 9/11. Pushtuns were the dominant ethnic group in the Afghan Kingdom from its emergence in the early eighteenth century until its demise in 1973. The leadership of the first Afghan "republic" (1973–78) was also Pushtun (indeed, the leader of the 1973 coup who became president was a member of the royal family). During the period of Marxist rule (1978–92), however, non-Pushtuns—especially Uzbeks and Tajiks—gained prominence in the government. The principal opposition that arose against the Marxist regime and Soviet occupation (and that was supported by America and others through Pakistan) was Pushtun, yet non-Pushtuns also opposed the Soviet occupation—especially a principally Tajik group in the Panjshir Valley led by Ahmed Shah Massoud. Pushtun and non-Pushtun opposition groups, however, usually did not work well together (indeed, there was much infighting even within the ranks of primarily Pushtun opposition movements based in Pakistan). The conflict in Afghanistan between the Soviet-backed Marxist regime and its opponents, then, was not just a conflict about ideology, but also an ethnic conflict (Ewans 2002).

Under Gorbachev, all Soviet forces were withdrawn from Afghanistan by early 1989. Owing to both support from Moscow (until the collapse of the Soviet Union at the end of 1991) and divisions among its opponents, the Marxist regime lasted until April 1992. Uzbeks and Tajiks remained predominant in the "Islamic state" that first replaced it. The Taliban, by contrast, was composed primarily of Pushtuns. Its seizure of power in most (but not all) of Afghanistan in 1996 represented a reassertion of the Pushtun dominance over the country that had ended under Marxist rule.

During the brief period in which it held power from 1996 to 2001, Taliban rule became unpopular not just with non-Pushtuns but with many Pushtuns as well. This fact greatly assisted the United States in rapidly bringing about the downfall of the Taliban regime in less than three months after 9/11. Mindful of Afghanistan's ethnic divisions, the Bush administration tried to balance its support between non-Pushtuns in the north and Pushtuns in the south. Furthermore, the United States did not reinstate Burhanuddin Rabbani, the Tajik president of the first Afghan Islamic republic that the Taliban ousted in 1996 but which, even though it retained control just in the northeast of the country, remained recognized by most other countries as the Afghan government. Instead, Washington pushed for the anti-Taliban Pushtun opposition leader, Hamid Karzai, to become president in an effort to appeal to the Pushtun south. The American-supported Afghan government's military, however, is dominated by northerners. As the *Economist* observed, "Less than 3% of recruits are from the troublesome Pushtun south, from where the Taliban draw most support. Few will sign up, fearing ruthless intimidation against government 'collaborators' and their families" ("Fixing the Unfixable" 2010).

As in Iraq, the U.S.-led intervention altered the existing ethnic balance in Afghanistan. Just as the Soviet intervention had done, the American intervention ended the Pushtun dominance that had existed under the monarchy and the first republic and which the Taliban had restored after the Soviets left. Unlike in Iraq, however, where the previously dominant Arab Sunnis are a minority (about 20%) and the Arab Shi'as are the majority (Minority Rights Group International 2011), the Pushtuns are the largest ethnic group in Afghanistan, constituting about 42 percent of the population (CIA 2011). Without an American military presence, the Pushtuns would be in a much stronger position to forcefully reestablish their dominance over Afghanistan than the Arab Sunnis would be to reestablish theirs in Iraq.

Despite the growth in the American troop presence in Afghanistan since late 2001, peace has not been established between Pushtuns and non-Pushtuns. Unless this changes, the prospects for stable democracy emerging in Afghanistan appear to be extremely poor, whether or not American forces remain there.

▼ ▼ ▼

Democratization and the Legacy
of History in the Muslim World

However well intentioned the Bush administration's efforts to democratize Afghanistan and Iraq after occupying them may have been, the preexisting ethnic and sectarian differences in these countries have proven to be a serious obstacle to achieving this goal, particularly since democratization upset the previous patterns of ethnic or sectarian dominance in them. The Bush administration, though, was not simply unlucky in selecting two countries whose internal divisions made them especially difficult to democratize. Instead of being exceptional, the sort of ethnic and sectarian differences present in Afghanistan and Iraq are quite typical of predominantly Muslim countries.

As with Afghanistan and Iraq before the U.S.-led interventions that attempted to introduce democracy, the governments of most predominantly Muslim countries are authoritarian. And also like in either Afghanistan or Iraq, democratization could well lead to the rise of secessionist demands on the part of regionally dominant minorities (as with the Kurds in northern Iraq), a weakening of the control previously exercised by a long-dominant group (as with the Pushtuns in Afghanistan), or even a transition from minority to majority rule (as in Iraq). A brief description of the ethnic and sectarian divisions in several predominantly Muslim countries, as well as an analysis of the effect of democratization on the existing power balance within them, will reveal just how widespread this phenomenon is.

Of course, some countries in the Muslim world (as well as elsewhere) are neither completely authoritarian nor fully democratic, but something in between that is hard to define. One such country is Pakistan, with an enormous population of over 170 million. According to the CIA World Factbook, Punjabis are the largest group in Pakistan (about 45%). Among the minorities are the Pushtuns (about 15.5%), Sindhis (14%), Sariakis (about 8%), Muhajirs (the Muslims—and their descendants—who fled from India to Pakistan in 1947 when the two countries were carved out of what had been British India; 7.5%), and Balochis (3.5%) (CIA 2011). The Punjabis, with a plurality, have been the dominant ethnicity and have long dominated the Pakistani security services. Other ethnic groups have often resented this. Secessionist movements have periodically arisen in Balochistan. The Pushtun-dominated Afghan monarchy used to encourage the secession of the Pushtun region of Pakistan. The Punjabis could probably maintain their dominance over Pakistan as a whole even if it were fully democratic. But if secession were ever put to a vote in the Pushtun, Balochi, or Sindhi regions of Pakistan, it is possible (though not certain) that majorities there might vote for it.

In Iran, Persians (according to the CIA World Factbook) are 51 percent of the population. Minority groups in Iran, which are concentrated in the border regions, include Azeris (24%), Kurds (7%), Arabs (3%), Balochis (2%), and Turkmen (2%). The CIA also claims that 89 percent of Iranians are Shi'a and 9 percent are Sunni. Especially since the breakup of the Soviet Union in 1991, Tehran has been fearful that a movement might arise among Iranian Azeris to secede from Iran and join independent (former Soviet) Azerbaijan. Similarly, the emergence of a de facto independent Kurdish state in northern Iraq has aroused concern that this might promote secessionism among Iranian Kurds. As in Pakistan, a violent Balochi opposition movement has also risen inside Iran. Genuine democratization in Iran, then, not only would threaten to replace the existing clerical order with a secular one but also could threaten the continuation of Persian dominance over non-Persian minorities, which could secede and either become independent or join neighboring states.

The overwhelming majority of the population of Turkey is Turkish (70%–75%). Although Kurds compose only 18 percent of the country's population (CIA 2011), the Turkish Armed Forces have been unable to eliminate a Kurdish separatist movement even after fighting it for decades. Just as Tehran does with regard to Iranian Kurds, Ankara fears that the emergence of the Kurdish Autonomous Region in neighboring Iraq might fuel secessionism among Turkish Kurds, which they might well vote in favor of if they were ever given the opportunity to do so. Turks themselves are also divided between the Turkish secular elite (who control the security services, which have deposed several of Turkey's elected governments and could well do so again in the future) and the increasingly religious populace. Full democratization would threaten the secular elite's privileged position in Turkey, as well as Turkish dominance over its Kurdish minority if the latter could ever force the holding of a referendum on secession.

Sunni Muslims are an overwhelming majority in Syria, where they make up about three-quarters of the country's population. It is, however, Syria's Alawite minority (estimated to make up as little as 7% of the population) that has long dominated the ruling Ba'th Party, the military, and the country as a whole (Nasir 2011). Democratization in Syria, should it ever occur, is highly likely to end Alawite minority rule and lead to Sunni majority rule.

Lebanon's Christian minority dominated the country up to its long civil war, which lasted from 1975 to 1990. According to Minority Rights Group International (2011), the principal sectarian groups in Lebanon are Sunni Muslims (28% of the population), Shi'a Muslims (also 28%), Maronite Christians (22%), Greek Orthodox (8%), Druze (6%), and Greek Catholics (4%). Since the end of the civil war, Lebanon has made significant progress toward democratization and reducing foreign influence—most notably in 2005, when a groundswell of local opposition led to the withdrawal of Syrian forces. Sadly, these developments have not ended division inside of Lebanon. At present, the main point of contention is between the powerful Shi'a organization Hezbollah (which receives support from both Syria and Iran and dominates southern Lebanon) and the Western-backed Sunnis and Christians. It must be emphasized, however, that Lebanon's sectarian communities are not monolithic; an important Christian faction led by Michel Aoun is currently aligned with Hezbollah (Dakroub 2011). As Lebanon's fractious history has shown, both alliances and enmities are highly fluid there.

The Hashemite monarchy that rules Jordan draws its support from (and mainly benefits) the Kingdom's Bedouin population. Bedouins, though, are estimated to make up only about one-third of Jordan's population, whereas Palestinians—who are Jordanian citizens—compose about one-half (Minority Rights Group International 2011). Democratization in Jordan, then, could result in empowering the Palestinians, disempowering the Bedouins, and perhaps deposing the Hashemite monarchy.

Saudi Arabia has four principal regions: Hejaz in the west, Najd in the center, Al Hasa (or the Eastern Province) in the east, and Asir in the southwest. The Saudi royal family hails from Najd; it built the Kingdom by conquering the other regions. The 2004 Saudi census indicated that 30 percent of the Saudi population lives in Najd, 32.2 percent in Hejaz, 15.5 percent in Al Hasa, and 18.8 percent in Asir (Yamani 2008, 156). While these figures do not necessarily correspond to regional identity, they indicate that democratization in Saudi Arabia could result in challenging the dominance of both the Saudi royal family and Najd. It might also raise the possibility of secession—especially in the oil-rich Eastern Province, where (according to Mai Yamani, a leading Saudi scholar) the Shi'a compose 75 percent of the population (Yamani 2008, 152).

In Bahrain, about 75 percent of its citizen population is Shi'a, while 25 percent of it is Sunni (Minority Rights Group International 2011). Like Iraq before the overthrow of Saddam Hussein's regime, Bahrain is a country where a Sunni minority (from which Bahrain's ruling family comes) rules over a restive Shi'a majority. Democratization in Bahrain would undoubtedly lead to

Shi'a majority rule—and probably the downfall of the Sunni ruling family also.

Oman is the only Muslim country where the rulers, including Sultan Qaboos (who has been in power since 1970), have traditionally been Ibadhis—a third branch of Islam distinct from both Sunnis and Shi'as. According to the CIA World Factbook, 75 percent of the Omani population is Ibadhi, while the remaining 25 percent is either Sunni, Shi'a, or Hindu. This suggests that while Oman is not a democracy, Sultan Qaboos at least hails from the majority community within Oman. Other sources, however, indicate that the Ibadhis form a much smaller percentage of the population. J. E. Peterson—one of the foremost Western scholars on Oman—estimated that 50 percent of Oman's indigenous population may be Sunni and only 45 percent Ibadhi (2004, 32). Dale F. Eickelman—also one of the foremost Western scholars on Oman—estimated that "roughly 50–55% of its citizen population is Sunni, 40–45% is Ibadhi, and less than 2% is Shi'a" (2001, 202). If indeed the Ibadhis are outnumbered by the Sunnis in Oman, democratization could lead to Sunnis replacing Ibadhis as the dominant community—and perhaps even to the downfall of the Ibadhi ruling family.

According to Minority Rights Group International, the population of Yemen consists of a Shafi'i Sunni majority (65%–70%) and a Zaidi Shi'a minority (30%–35%). What since 1990 has been united Yemen was previously two countries: North Yemen and South Yemen. Under both the monarchy (1918–62) and the republic (1962–90), Zaidi Shi'as ruled the North. As a result of unification in 1990 and the civil war of 1994, the predominantly Shafi'i Sunnis in the much less populous South came under the domination of northerners. Democratization in Yemen could lead to Shafi'i Sunnis displacing Zaidi Shi'as as the dominant group in Yemen as a whole, or to the reestablishment of the South's independence.

Sudan is a country with extraordinary ethnic and sectarian diversity. According to the CIA World Factbook, Sudan's population (before the independence of South Sudan in July 2011) was 52 percent African (black) and 39 percent Arab. Once again, it has been the minority—the Arabs in this case—that has dominated the country. In addition, the pre-breakup Sudanese population was estimated to be 70 percent Sunni (concentrated in the north), 5 percent Christian, and 25 percent followers of indigenous beliefs (concentrated in the south). The black southerners fought so long and hard for independence from the Arab-dominated north that the latter finally agreed to allow a referendum on this to be held in the south in January 2011. In it, the southerners overwhelmingly voted in favor of independence—a result that the Sudanese government in Khartoum agreed to honor. There are also, however, other secessionist movements, including the well-known one in Darfur (western Sudan) and less well-known ones in eastern and northern Sudan. So far, Khartoum has not been willing to even consider the possibility of their secession. These other conflicts also appear to have an Arab versus African component. The secessionists, however, are far from unified and often divide along tribal or other bases.

The patterns of ethnic and sectarian dominance in other predominantly Muslim countries in the Middle East, North Africa, the Sahel, Central Asia, and Southeast Asia could also be described, but the point made for the countries already discussed applies to many of them too: democratization could lead to the disruption of existing patterns of ethnic and/or sectarian dominance in them, which in turn could lead either to minorities seeking secession or to minority rule being replaced by majority rule.

How did these existing patterns of ethnic and sectarian dominance emerge in so many predominantly Muslim countries? This is an interesting question that would require a separate research project to address fully and therefore cannot be addressed in detail here. The following, however, should be noted: First, the potential for democratization to disrupt existing patterns of ethnic and sectarian dominance is not unique to the Muslim world; it has already manifested itself—or could do so—in many countries around the world. Second, patterns of dominance established by force in the past have often been maintained despite demographic change. Third, European powers often found local minorities to be willing partners in the colonial enterprise since this granted them a degree of power and prestige that they would not have enjoyed otherwise. Further, these privileged minorities were often able to take full power themselves after the departure of the European colonial administration. Finally, what is of concern for this study is not how existing patterns of ethnic and/or sectarian dominance in predominantly Muslim countries came about, but how they affect—and are affected by—the War on Terror.

One clear implication is that, contrary to President Bush's expectation that its promotion in the greater Middle East would lead to peace, the prospect that democratization might lead not just to the election of radical Islamists but also to secession and/or the overthrow of privileged minorities in so many Muslim countries made it appear highly destabilizing and undesirable to all too many. Democratization in the greater Middle East, in other words, portended the downfall of existing regimes, the collapse of existing states, and conflict within and among them. Not surprisingly, then, governments and privileged groups in this region have resisted democratization because they anticipated that pursuing it would lead to losing control over or the breakup of their countries (or both).

This is not to say that democratization in predominantly Muslim (or non-Muslim) countries with significant ethnic and/or sectarian differences cannot be undertaken successfully. Indonesia— the most populous country in the Muslim world—has made the transition from an authoritarian military regime to a working, moderate democracy that has so far forestalled secessionist efforts (with the exception of the anomalous case of predominantly Catholic East Timor) and kept at bay the forces of Islamist extremism.

The United States and its Western allies, then, should not refrain from promoting democracy in predominantly Muslim countries just because it could lead to instability in them. As Iraq and Afghanistan have painfully demonstrated, however, the attempt to forcefully impose democracy upon a nation based on the assumption that the people there want it can be highly costly, as well as unsuccessful, when ethnic and sectarian divisions are omnipresent. Indeed, it is noteworthy that Indonesia's successful transition to democracy occurred without the aid of external intervention, whereas East Timor's independence from Indonesia—which was supported by Western military intervention—has been less successful and its democratization efforts have been fraught with difficulty.

All this suggests two conclusions: One is that because of the many ethnic and sectarian differences within them, the democratization of predominantly Muslim countries is likely to be more complicated than many in the West and the Muslim world itself would like. The other is that America and its allies might more effectively promote democratization in the Muslim world through the slow process of supporting indigenous democratization movements that seek to reach across ethnic and sectarian divides instead of through direct intervention that eliminates authoritarian regimes before democratization movements have arisen that could ameliorate and overcome these divisions.

▼ ▼ ▼

Assessing the Obama Strategy

When he was running for president in 2008, Barack Obama argued that the manner in which the Bush administration had prosecuted the War on Terror had inflicted more harm on America than good. Obama was especially critical of the Bush administration's costly intervention in Iraq (which he opposed) for unnecessarily reducing the resources available for the war in Afghanistan (which he then supported). Nor had the U.S.-led interventions in Iraq and Afghanistan prevented the spread of radical Islamist activity elsewhere. Further, he argued, the Bush approach to the War on Terror had harmed America's relations with not only the Muslim world but its Western allies. Finally, it was not cost-effective for the United States to spend so much of its resources to produce such meager results. All this was—in both his view and that of many others—highly counterproductive for the United States and for American foreign policy. Upon becoming president in January 2009, then, Obama implemented a strategy regarding the War on Terror that was the opposite of the Bush administration's in several respects.

Whereas Bush had pursued a unilateralist foreign policy, Obama was determined to pursue a multilateral one. It was Bush's

unilateralism—especially about the use of force—that had alienated America's allies and the Muslim world. Indeed, there were
many who claimed that American foreign policy under Bush was
more of a threat to the security of others than was Al Qaeda
(Vogelgesang 2008, 104). The United States clearly did not benefit from such an image. Obama, then, insisted on pursuing a
multilateral policy in conjunction with America's allies and partners. This would at least improve America's relations with them.

While Bush had intervened in and occupied Iraq, Obama was
determined to withdraw American forces from there. More than
any other action, Bush's decision to intervene in Iraq without UN
Security Council authorization had alienated much of the world,
distracted attention from the war in Afghanistan, unleashed com-
munal warfare in Iraq, and did not contribute much of anything
to the defeat of Al Qaeda. Withdrawing from Iraq, it was expected, would improve U.S. relations with its friends and allies
and provide additional resources for the war in Afghanistan and
the struggle against Al Qaeda. The Bush administration's 2007–8
troop surge, it was grudgingly admitted, did improve the security
situation in Iraq. This, however, was seen as a factor that would
allow the United States to leave Iraq.

Whereas Bush had called for and even sought to democratize
the greater Middle East, Obama made it clear that this was not
his goal. In his June 4, 2009, speech in Cairo, Obama did note
that "governments that protect . . . rights are ultimately more
stable, successful and secure." But in speaking about democracy,
he also stated, "No system of government can or should be imposed upon one nation by any other." Bush had earlier stated
that the lack of democracy led to instability. Although Obama
couched his statement in the language of cultural sensitivity, it
implicitly recognized that externally promoted democratization
such as Bush had attempted could also lead to instability.

While Bush strongly supported Hamid Karzai as the president of Afghanistan, Obama made clear practically upon taking
office that he regarded Karzai's corrupt, inefficient government
as an important cause of the growing problems that the United
States was facing in that country. There was some irony in this:

Bush called for democratization but supported an undemocratic (albeit elected) Afghan president, while Obama announced he would not push for democratization but criticized Karzai for not being democratic. Still, with American forces so heavily engaged in Afghanistan, a higher standard for that country compared with ones where they were not engaged was understandable.

Another aspect of Obama's foreign policy that was different from Bush's involved the Israeli-Palestinian conflict. Whereas Bush gave complete, uncritical support to Israel, Obama called upon Israel to modify its behavior toward the Palestinians. In his Cairo speech, he bluntly stated that "the United States does not accept the legitimacy of continued Israeli settlements. . . . It is time for these settlements to stop." Although Bush behaved as if the two issues were not strongly related to each other, Obama seems well aware that the state of Israeli-Palestinian relations has a strong impact—for better or for worse—on how successfully the United States conducts the War on Terror.

Finally, while Bush placed a higher priority on prosecuting the War on Terror than on domestic and other foreign policy issues, Obama places a higher priority on issues other than the war. The severe global financial crisis that greeted Obama upon entering office forced this change in U.S. priorities to some extent; however, Obama has indicated that he saw continued large-scale American military intervention in Iraq and Afghanistan as hindering the pursuit of his other domestic and international goals.

How successful has Obama's changed approach toward the War on Terror been? One positive development has been the improvement in America's ties with many governments that had opposed the Bush administration's unilateralism—especially its intervention in Iraq without the approval of the UN Security Council. Obama also set in motion the U.S. military withdrawal from Iraq that got under way in 2010. Further, he established a time frame for a U.S. withdrawal from Afghanistan to begin in mid-2011 and be completed by the end of 2014.

Nevertheless, old problems remain while some new ones have cropped up with regard to the War on Terror. As Iraq and especially Afghanistan have shown, these conflicts are far from over.

Further, the Obama administration's criticism of Hamid Karzai did not result in his adoption of the reforms that the United States sought, but in his truculently opposing them and even stating that he would be compelled to join the Taliban (Rosenberg and Zahori 2010). Nor has Obama succeeded in getting the Israelis to make any serious concessions toward the Palestinians, or vice versa, in order to reach an Israeli-Palestinian peace settlement.

Further, although Osama bin Laden was killed in Abbottabad, Pakistan, by U.S. forces on May 2, 2011, Al Qaeda and its affiliates remain active. Radical Islamists appear to be gaining strength in Pakistan, Yemen, and Somalia. The brief burst of enthusiastic public support in the Muslim world that Obama enjoyed when he first became president has subsequently declined markedly.

The Obama administration came into office convinced that it was the Bush administration's policies toward the War on Terror that had damaged America's image in and relations with the Muslim world. Obama sought to change this through reversing many of his predecessor's policies and reaching out to the Muslim world in his Cairo speech and on other occasions. Yet despite his efforts, the War on Terror continues, and Washington must deal with it.

The next two parts of this book will examine two problems that the Obama administration and one or more of its successors will have to formulate policy toward: how to minimize the damage and even take advantage of the opportunities that may arise as a result of the U.S. withdrawals from Iraq and Afghanistan, and how to go about attempting to decouple regional and local conflicts in the Muslim world, resulting from the legacy of history discussed earlier, from the overall War on Terror.

Opportunities
after Withdrawal

▼ ▼ ▼

Consequences of Withdrawing from Iraq and Afghanistan

Whatever the strengths and weaknesses of the Obama strategy toward the War on Terror, one aspect of it is clear: the president is determined to withdraw American forces from both Iraq and Afghanistan. American combat forces have already left Iraq. The remaining "support" troops were due to leave by the end of 2011. And although Obama sent an additional thirty thousand troops to Afghanistan, he also stated firmly that he intended to begin drawing down the U.S. troop presence there in mid-2011—even though the generals he himself appointed opposed this.

Was this the right decision? That is not the question that will be discussed here. What is more important to note is that Obama's decision appears to be firm and is likely to set the course of American foreign policy for some time to come. For once the withdrawals have been completed—or even just begun in earnest—it is highly unlikely that they will be reversed even by a subsequent Republican administration. While Republican candidates for office may denounce Obama's decision, a Republican administration is hardly likely to renew military interventions that the American public no longer supports and wants to see ended.

The more important question to explore is, what are the implications of the American decision to withdraw from Iraq and Afghanistan? Forecasting, of course, is hazardous. There are, however, some highly likely consequences of this decision that should be noted.

First and foremost among these is that the United States will have less influence in these two countries as it withdraws from them. If the United States was hard-pressed to control events in them even with a large military presence, it will obviously be less able to do so with little or no such presence. Specifically, withdrawal of its troops from Iraq means that the United States will be unable to prevent the outbreak of renewed sectarian violence there. Withdrawing its troops from Afghanistan means that the United States will be unable to prevent an even greater resurgence of the Taliban than has been occurring while American troops are still there.

Another likely consequence of the United States withdrawing from Iraq and Afghanistan will be (indeed, already is) the growth in the perception that American power and influence are on the decline in the greater Middle East (and perhaps elsewhere). Just as when it withdrew its forces from Indochina at the beginning of 1973, the United States will be seen, both internationally and domestically, as entering a period in which it is less willing and able to intervene abroad. This, of course, will be welcome to some (mainly America's adversaries, but also some of its resentful "friends") and unwelcome to others (mainly the beneficiaries of interventions that are ending, as well as those who now fear that the United States will not protect them from their adversaries).

A third consequence is likely to result from the previous two: American withdrawals from Iraq and Afghanistan combined with the increased perception that the United States is now less likely to intervene or re-intervene may serve to convince America's adversaries that they have succeeded in driving the United States out of these two countries and that they may succeed in driving it out of others as well. Among those that may persuade themselves of this include the Islamic Republic of Iran, Al Qaeda, and Al Qaeda's various affiliates in different countries. America withdrawing from Iraq and Afghanistan could also embolden other countries to increase their involvement in them—especially Pakistan in Afghanistan, and Iran in Iraq (and possibly Afghanistan as well).

A fourth consequence, ironically, may be that some of America's allies in the region become less amenable to U.S. influence. If they perceive the United States as being less willing and able to defend them, then they may decide that they need to make alternative security arrangements. These could range from preemptively attacking their opponents, to attempting to reach a modus vivendi with them, to seeking out other allies either in addition to or in place of the United States. Whether any of these alternative security arrangements would prove successful if attempted, of course, remains to be seen. Just the attempt to implement any of them, however, could increase the volatility of an already unstable region.

Finally, an American withdrawal from Iraq and Afghanistan will do nothing to ease the region's many other problems, including the Israeli-Palestinian dispute, Indo-Pakistani hostility, or the rise of Islamic radicalism in Pakistan, Yemen, Somalia, and elsewhere. Of course, the presence of American forces in Iraq and Afghanistan has done nothing to ease them either. In other words, there are many problems in the region that are likely to continue no matter what happens in Iraq and Afghanistan.

It is not inevitable, of course, that all of these problems will emerge following an American withdrawal from Iraq and Afghanistan. Some, though, probably cannot be avoided, especially the reduction of U.S. influence in Iraq and Afghanistan and the growth in the perception that American influence in the region is declining. The emergence of just these two problems alone will lead to a more challenging foreign policy environment for the United States. Yet even if all five of the problems outlined here emerge, America and its allies will still have options and opportunities for limiting the spread of Islamic radicalism and for contributing to the erosion of its influence in those places where it has become politically dominant. For in addition to the trends outlined here that would serve to weaken American influence, there are three other trends that could emerge to strengthen it: regional opposition to Islamic radicals, intolerant behavior on the part of Islamic radicals believing themselves victorious, and divisions among Islamic radicals. The emergence of any or (especially) all of these trends would provide America and its allies with ample opportunity to work with others against radical Islamic forces. The likelihood of these three trends emerging will each be examined in turn.

▼ ▼ ▼

Regional Opposition

Many fear (while others hope) that American withdrawals from
Iraq and Afghanistan will be followed by Islamic radical forces
taking over these two countries and then spreading their influence to neighboring ones. The U.S. withdrawal from Iraq, some
believe, will lead to Iran working with Iraqi Shi'a forces to not only
dominate Iraq but also threaten the Sunni-led governments in
neighboring Kuwait, Saudi Arabia, and Jordan, as well as others
farther away. Similarly, an American withdrawal from Afghanistan, it is feared, will lead to the Pakistani-backed Taliban return-
ing to power in Afghanistan and then supporting the spread of
radical Islamic revolution to Central Asia and perhaps even the
predominantly Muslim regions of Russia.

Indeed, the fear of Islamic revolutionaries taking over in any
one country is not just what this would mean for that particular
country (as well as for its relations with Western and other governments), but also what it means for the prospects of spreading
Islamic revolution to other countries. This fear, of course, is
similar to that which existed during the Cold War: the success of
Marxist revolutionaries in coming to power in any one country
was seen as increasing the prospects for Marxist revolution in

neighboring ones. This fear also existed with regard to Arab nationalist revolution, especially in the late 1950s and early 1960s.

The fear—then and now—is not just of revolution in one country but revolutionary contagion spreading from one country to others. During the Cold War, this notion was popularly referred to as the domino theory. But how realistic is this fear at present? While what happened in the past is not predestined to occur again, examining the past can help us to identify the various forces that promoted and opposed the spread of revolution then and to ponder whether similar forces may be at work now.

In both the Arab nationalist and the Marxist-Leninist revolutionary waves, this fear of revolutionary contagion appeared justified—for a time. After Nasser came to power in Egypt in 1952, he proclaimed his vision of uniting the Arab world, and his seeming victory over Britain, France, and Israel in the 1956 Suez Crisis did help spread new Arab nationalist revolutions to other countries. Arab nationalists seized power in Syria and Iraq in 1958, in North Yemen and Algeria in 1962, and in Libya and Sudan in 1969. But while Arab nationalist forces came to power in several Arab countries, they did not come to power in others, and they certainly did not unite the Arab world into one country. One reason for this is that the West opposed further expansion of Arab nationalism through American intervention in Lebanon and British intervention in Jordan in 1958. Additionally, regional forces opposed Arab nationalist efforts, including conservative monarchies such as Saudi Arabia and Morocco and the Marxists in South Yemen (Kerr 1971).

Similarly, the U.S. withdrawal from Indochina in 1973 was followed by Marxist takeovers in South Vietnam, Laos, and Cambodia in 1975. But Marxism did not spread to Thailand or other countries in Southeast Asia as the proponents of the domino theory had warned. Marxist revolutionaries, of course, did seize power in several other regions of the Third World during the 1970s, including Ethiopia, Portugal's African colonies (Angola, Mozambique, and Guinea-Bissau), Afghanistan, Nicaragua, and even Grenada; however, they did not succeed in coming to power anywhere else in the Third World. While American foreign policy did play some role in this (especially after the 1979 Soviet invasion of Afghanistan), the knowledge that the American Congress and public were unwilling to undertake any more counterinsurgency operations after the experience of Indochina undoubtedly served to encourage Marxist revolutionaries, not deter them. By contrast, regional powers—either with or without U.S. support—played a crucial role in containing or even damaging pro-Soviet Marxist regimes in their neighborhood. These included white-ruled South Africa's efforts against Marxist Angola; Chinese and Thai cooperation against the pro-Hanoi Marxist regime that Vietnam installed in Cambodia after its 1978 invasion; and the actions undertaken by Pakistan, Iran, Saudi Arabia, China, and others—in addition to the United States—in support of the Afghan mujahideen fighting against the Soviet occupation of their country (Rodman 1994).

Regional opposition also arose to prevent radical Islamic regimes from exporting revolution to other countries prior to 9/11. In 1980, Iraq attacked Iran under Saddam Hussein's mistaken assumption that he could take advantage of Iranian weakness. But after Iranian forces expelled Saddam's forces and then moved into Iraq, several countries aided Baghdad in order to prevent Iran from overrunning Iraq and the much weaker Arab states bordering it (Walt 1996, 238–68). Similarly, neighboring countries strongly resisted the efforts of the Islamic regime that came to power in Sudan in 1989 to export revolution (Mantzikos 2010). Finally, both Russia and Iran worked to prevent the Taliban from overrunning all of Afghanistan from even before 1996, when the Taliban seized control of most of the country, until late 2001, when the United States took it upon itself to drive the Taliban out of power (Khalilzad and Byman 2000). And since 9/11, of course, many governments—whether in the West, the Muslim world, or elsewhere—have worked against Al Qaeda and other Islamic radical groups. They have done this not so much to help the United States as to protect themselves against the threat that radical Islamic groups pose to their own security or even survival.

Following the American withdrawals from Iraq and Afghanistan, then, it would not be surprising if regional opposition arose both to prevent Iran from dominating Iraq and to prevent the Pakistani-backed Taliban from dominating Afghanistan. Indeed, it would be highly surprising if such regional opposition did not arise. Some signs of it are already visible. In Afghanistan, for example, Russia, India, and Iran are all reportedly working with one another and with non-Pushtun groups that (like them) oppose the Taliban's return to power (Dalrymple 2010). And although the Saudi government fired him for saying so in a 2006 *Washington Post* op-ed piece, Saudi analyst Nawaf Obaid's prediction that the Kingdom would assist the Sunni Arabs in Iraq if the United States withdrew appears to be coming true. A similar reaction can be expected anywhere else that Islamic radicals seize power: regional powers and neighboring states will work to prevent the new regime from exporting revolution.

All this is important because, in the past, regional opposition has often proven to be an important barrier to the spread of revolution from one country to its neighbors. It is also likely to pose a similar obstacle to the spread of revolution in the future.

▼ ▼ ▼

Radical Repression

Whatever popular support they may enjoy before coming to power or just afterward, radical Islamic revolutionaries have quickly proven themselves to be harsh authoritarian rulers wherever they have come to power. The Islamic revolutionaries who have ruled in Iran since 1979, in Sudan since 1989, in most of Afghanistan from 1996 to 2001, in parts of Somalia since 1999, and in parts of Iraq during the mid-2000s all imposed dictatorial regimes.

The imposition of authoritarian rule, of course, is not something unique to Islamic revolutionaries, but common to non-democratic revolutionaries in general. Despite all their promises both before and after coming to power about what ideal societies they would build, Marxist-Leninist and Arab nationalist revolutionaries ruled in an oppressive, authoritarian manner. Sometimes this led to armed internal opposition against the revolutionary regime. But even where it did not (or where this failed), authoritarian rule resulted in a corrosive disillusionment with the revolutionary regime and its ideology. An odd dichotomy then arose: a particular brand of revolutionary ideology could become more popular in countries where it had not come to power and its promises of a better life after ousting the incumbent regime were still believed than in countries where it had come to power and its performance had proven increasingly disappointing over time.

Is this a problem that radical Islamic revolutionaries could overcome in the future? In order to do so, they would have to acknowledge that their own authoritarian behavior generated opposition—whether active or passive—against them. Even if they acknowledged this, however, it would be very difficult to prevent disillusionment with the regime and its ideology from growing in the societies they rule, for two reasons:

First, nondemocratic revolutionary regimes—especially when they first come to power and for many years afterward—usually do not succeed at promoting prosperity. Instead, as Forrest D. Colburn explained in *The Vogue of Revolution in Poor Countries* (1994), they usually oversee increasing poverty—even in countries that are rich in petroleum such as Iran and Angola. There have, of course, been exceptions. China is a case in which a communist regime successfully oversaw capitalist economic development; however, it took decades and the death of the first revolutionary leader, Mao Tse-tung, before Beijing recognized the need for integration into the world market. And then it took further decades for China to fully achieve this. None of the Islamic radicals—whether already long in power or still seeking it—appear to regard following China's path to economic prosperity as even desirable.

Second, although transnational revolutionary ideologies promise to overcome the ethnic and sectarian divisions existing in countries they come to rule, they usually reinforce them instead. The revolutionary leadership either starts out being dominated by one particular sect or ethnic group or becomes so as power struggles play out and the winners increasingly rely on those they trust most: their own ethnic and/or sectarian group. Shi'a Persians, for example, dominate the Islamic Republic of Iran, as well as the non-Persians and (most especially) non-Shi'as within it. The Arab minority has dominated the Islamic regime in Sudan. Pushtuns were the dominant group when the Taliban ruled Afghanistan from 1996 to 2001 and would be the dominant force once again if the Taliban returns to power there. Just as the ethnic and sectarian divisions that are the legacy of history in so many predominantly Muslim countries pose an important obstacle to democratization in them (as discussed earlier), this same legacy of history poses an important obstacle for Islamic revolutionary regimes that claim to overcome these divisions but in reality do not.

Of course, nondemocratic revolutionary regimes usually do not acknowledge—even to themselves—that their actions may be the cause of their own problems. They tend to blame others for these and to view all who disagree with them as enemies who must be isolated, defeated, or eliminated. Their doing so, however, only serves to make their rule less popular, thus necessitating further authoritarian measures to keep the revolutionary regime in power, which can in turn foster more opposition—and on and on in a vicious circle.

The United States and many other governments do not want to see Islamic authoritarian revolution spread to any more countries. But if Islamic revolution does spread to other countries, their intolerant nature will generate various forms of domestic opposition against them over time—as has occurred with the Islamic revolutionary regimes that have already come to power. And just as the unpopularity of the authoritarian governments in the Muslim world that are allied to the United States is a vulnerability that Islamic revolutionaries have exploited (and will continue to exploit), the unpopular nature of authoritarian Islamic revolutionary regimes is a vulnerability that America and its allies can also exploit.

▼ ▼ ▼

Rifts among the Radicals

If serious disputes arose between Islamic revolutionary actors, America and others might be able to exploit them. But will such serious disputes arise? Some in the United States and elsewhere—especially those who engage in "worst-case analysis"—believe that this possibility is simply too good to be true and that it would be naive to expect it. But serious disputes between Islamic radicals have occurred in the past, are occurring now, and are likely to continue occurring in the future.

The most serious ongoing disputes between Islamic radical actors are those between Sunnis and Shi'as. Radical Sunnis in particular are virulently opposed to Shi'ism, which they view as a form of apostasy (Haykel 2010). Radical Sunni and radical Shi'a movements in Iraq did not do anything to halt the sectarian conflict there; indeed, they did much to egg it on (Bergen 2011, 163–68). While less publicized, radical Sunni groups have made several violent attacks against the Shi'a-dominated government inside Iran over the past few years (Erdbrink 2008; Bozorgmehr 2010). In Lebanon, radical Sunni groups have felt threatened by the rising power and influence of the radical Shi'a movement Hezbollah (Abdel-Latif 2008). In addition, the Al Qaeda–affiliated

Abdullah Azzam Brigades organization has denounced Hezbollah for being Syria's "Shiite agent in Lebanon" (Blanford 2011). In Yemen, the Shi'a rebels in the north of the country—the Houthis—are at odds with Al Qaeda in the Arabian Peninsula and other Yemeni Sunnis (Ali 2011). And in Pakistan, radical Sunnis have perpetrated numerous attacks on the minority Shi'a community there (Lawson 2011).

The Sunni-Shi'a rift, though, is not the only division within the Islamic radical community. The leadership of Egypt's Muslim Brotherhood (a Sunni movement) has been highly critical of Al Qaeda for being so violent (Lynch 2010). Al Qaeda and Hamas—which is an offshoot of the Egyptian Muslim Brotherhood—are bitterly antagonistic toward each other (Paz 2010). Tensions also exist between Iraqi Shi'as and Iran (Pollock and Ali 2010).

That serious divisions exist between Islamic revolutionary actors should not be regarded as unusual or exceptional. Indeed, their occurrence is quite similar to the divisions that plagued both Arab nationalists and Marxist-Leninists in the past.

While it was the goal of the Arab nationalists to unite the Arab world into a large single country, one of the most serious obstacles to achieving this goal was that Arab nationalist leaders and regimes in different countries often fiercely opposed each other. Upon seizing power in Syria in 1958, the Ba'th Party there promptly entered a union with Nasser's Egypt called the United Arab Republic; however, in 1961 the Ba'th Party pulled Syria out of the UAR amidst much acrimony and recrimination. The Arab Nationalist Free Officers who seized power in Iraq in 1958 fell out with Nasser almost immediately. The Iraqi branch of the Ba'th Party eventually seized power in Baghdad. But the Iraqi Ba'th regime and the Syrian Ba'th regime were constantly at odds with each other. Thus, although Arab nationalist regimes arose in seven Arab countries (Egypt, Syria, Iraq, Algeria, North Yemen, Sudan, and Libya), the internecine rivalry that arose among them—especially among the three most powerful (Egypt, Syria, and Iraq)—was an important factor preventing them from achieving their common goal of uniting the Arab world (Kerr 1971).

Between the end of World War II and the collapse of communism, there were several serious rifts among Marxist-Leninist actors. The most famous of these was the Sino-Soviet rift. But other rifts also developed, including ones between the USSR and Yugoslavia, between Yugoslavia and Albania, between the USSR and Albania, and between Vietnam and Khmer Rouge–ruled Cambodia. After the Sino-Soviet rift developed, Communist parties in many countries split into pro-Moscow and pro-Beijing branches. In addition to being anti-Soviet, the Communist regime in Albania became anti-Chinese in 1979. Although ostensibly Maoist, the Peruvian Marxist movement, Sendero Luminoso, was highly critical not just of the USSR but of post-Maoist China as well (Katz 1997).

Furthermore, in both the Marxist-Leninist and the Arab nationalist cases, some regimes that shared the same or a similar anti-Western revolutionary ideology became so hostile toward each other that this contributed to a rapprochement between one or more revolutionary regimes and the United States. In other words, revolutionary regimes came to see a fellow revolutionary regime as more of a threat than the previously reviled United States. Examples of this include (1) Yugoslavia under Tito, who turned to the West for support after falling out with Stalin in the late 1940s; (2) China under Mao, who developed cooperative relations with the United States in the early 1970s after the Sino-Soviet rift had intensified to the point of conflict along their common border in the late 1960s; and (3) Egypt under Sadat, who preferred cooperation with the United States and even Israel to continued solidarity with Arab nationalist (and other Arab) regimes against them.

Could something like this happen with Islamic revolutionary actors? Could a rift between two of them grow so intense that one of them would turn to the once hated United States or some other non-Muslim power for support against the other? Though not well known in the West, there has already been one instance of this scenario occurring relatively recently in Afghanistan. One of the most effective fighters resisting the Soviet occupation of Afghanistan during the 1980s was the Tajik Islamic warrior Ahmad

Shah Massoud, who was based in the Panjshir Valley. After Soviet forces withdrew in 1988–89 and the Marxist regime it left behind fell in 1992, Massoud became the defense minister in the newly declared Islamic State of Afghanistan. But after this regime (in which non-Pushtun northerners predominated) was ousted from the capital by the Taliban (dominated by Pushtuns) in 1996, Massoud returned to the Panjshir Valley to resist the Taliban from there. The fact that they had fought against each other in the 1980s proved to be no obstacle to Moscow providing arms to Massoud, or to Massoud accepting them, from the mid-1990s until his assassination two days before 9/11 (Risen 1998; Shermatova 2001).

There was also another occasion in which this might have happened. War almost broke out between Iran and the Taliban regime in Afghanistan in 1998 after nine Iranian diplomats in Afghanistan were seized and executed by either the Taliban or groups linked to them. As tensions rose, Tehran reportedly moved seventy thousand Revolutionary Guards toward its border with Afghanistan (Ewans 2002, 274). If war between them had erupted, and especially if this war had been prolonged, either Tehran or the Taliban may have put aside hostility toward the West long enough to accept Western military assistance, especially if it were losing. But since this scenario did not arise, it is impossible to determine whether either Tehran or the Taliban would have taken this step.

Whether hostility between Islamic radicals led—or might have led—to a rapprochement between one or more such actors and a previously reviled status quo power in the past, of course, is far less important than an assessment of the possibility that something like this could occur now. At present, it must be said, no Islamic revolutionary government or opposition movement appears likely to ally with the United States or any other non-Muslim power against a rival Islamic revolutionary actor. Neither Iran, Al Qaeda, the Taliban, Hamas, Hezbollah, Al Qaeda in the Arabian Peninsula, nor any other such actor appears willing to either improve relations with Washington or be amenable to any American overtures (should they be forthcoming) for this.

But as previous experience suggests, rapprochements between status quo powers and revolutionary actors cannot be ruled out. Although such rapprochements have happened in the past and thus could happen again, history also suggests that rifts among revolutionary actors may have to exist for years before one of them is willing to ally with a status quo power against the other. The Sino-Soviet rift began in the 1950s, but it was not until the early 1970s that a Sino-American rapprochement began. Similarly, Egypt had poor relations with Arab nationalist regimes in Iraq (starting in 1958) and Syria (starting in 1961) long before Cairo developed friendly relations first with the United States and then with Israel in the 1970s.

Further, the passage of time alone is usually not sufficient to bring about a rapprochement between a revolutionary regime and a status quo power. Something else may have to occur that encourages this development. A leadership change in a revolutionary regime can facilitate rapprochement. The Egyptian-American rapprochement, for example, occurred after Sadat replaced Nasser. This, however, may not be necessary: previously anti-American revolutionary leaders such as Mao and Qaddafi were still in power when China and Libya began rapprochements with the United States in the early 1970s and the early 2000s, respectively.

Another circumstance that can facilitate a rapprochement between a revolutionary regime and a status quo power is when the former comes to see another revolutionary actor as more of a threat than the status quo power it previously identified as the principal enemy. The growing Soviet and Chinese perceptions of each other as a more serious threat than the United States helped motivate both Moscow and Beijing to pursue rapprochement with the United States in the early 1970s. What allowed such a perception to arise, of course, was the underlying perception not just in Moscow and Beijing but more generally (including in the United States) that American power was declining as a result of "imperial overstretch," as Paul Kennedy phrased it (1989, 515).

There is certainly no guarantee that divisions among Islamic revolutionary actors will emerge or become exacerbated as a result of the increased perception that American power is declining. But given the uncompromising nature of Islamic revolutionary leaders (indeed, nondemocratic ones generally), this could well happen. It hardly seems coincidental that after the initiation of the American withdrawal from Iraq and President Obama's announcement that the United States would begin withdrawing from Afghanistan in mid-2011, the virulently anti-American Al Qaeda in the Arabian Peninsula leader Anwar al-Awlaki issued a warning to Sunni Arabs about the spread of Iranian influence into the Arabian Peninsula (Fisher 2010). Indeed, Iran could not be seen as such a threat by al-Awlaki unless he believed that American power in the region is on the decline.

The exacerbation of the Al Qaeda–Iran rift, or of others between Islamic revolutionary actors, will not necessarily lead to one or another of them turning to the United States for help against the other, especially in the near term. But if any Islamic revolutionary actor comes to fear that its very survival is threatened by another such actor, it could well happen. If and when it does, this is an opportunity that America and its allies should be prepared to take advantage of.

▼ ▼ ▼

Withdrawal Need Not Be Defeat

Many have warned that if the United States withdraws from Iraq and Afghanistan, the American-backed efforts to foster democratic government in both are likely to fail, Islamist radicals are likely to seize control of significant portions (if not all) of both countries, and some neighboring states hostile to American interests (especially Iran) are likely to take advantage of the situation. Furthermore, American withdrawal from these two conflicts after sacrificing so many lives, spending so much money, and devoting so much time to them without achieving victory cannot help but encourage Islamist and other radicals elsewhere and weaken America's standing in the world. Yet for the United States to remain as deeply committed as it has been for so many years in either conflict (much less both) is untenable both politically and economically not just for the Obama administration but even for a future Republican one, especially since there is no guarantee that continuing a high-level U.S. military commitment will prove more successful or less costly than has been the case so far. In other words, while there will undoubtedly be negative consequences for America if U.S. forces withdraw from Afghanistan and Iraq, there will also be negative consequences if they remain but are unable to achieve significantly better results than they have so far.

The position that the United States finds itself in now is reminiscent of the position it was in during the early 1970s. Back then, the United States had become bogged down militarily not only in South Vietnam after many years fighting there but also in Laos and Cambodia. The American war effort had become highly unpopular in many countries throughout the world, including the United States itself. Many warned that an American military withdrawal from Indochina would lead to negative consequences for the United States there and elsewhere, as well as for America's standing in the world more generally.

Political and economic conditions inside the United States, however, forced the Nixon administration to withdraw American forces from Indochina by the beginning of 1973. And many of the negative consequences that were warned of by those who wanted America to continue its war effort in Indochina did indeed come to pass. Communist forces overran South Vietnam, Cambodia, and Laos in the spring of 1975. Further, the unwillingness of the American public and Congress to undertake military interventions elsewhere for fear of "another Vietnam" only encouraged Marxist revolutionaries—and their supporters in Moscow, Havana, and elsewhere—to seize the moment. During the 1970s, Marxist revolutionaries succeeded in coming to power in several other countries, including Ethiopia, Guinea-Bissau, Mozambique, Angola, Afghanistan, and Nicaragua. Powerful Marxist insurgencies appeared likely to seize power in still other countries during the 1980s, including El Salvador and elsewhere in Central America, Peru, and the Philippines. America's alliances appeared to be in tatters. There was a general sense that American power and influence were on the decline while those of the Soviet Union were on the rise.

By the early 1990s, however, the situation had completely changed. Soviet forces, which had invaded Afghanistan in 1979, withdrew from there in 1989 without having defeated the anti-Soviet insurgency. The communist regimes of Eastern Europe that were allied to Moscow all collapsed in late 1989. Most Third

World Marxist regimes either collapsed or realigned themselves with the West. At the end of 1991, the Soviet Union itself broke apart into fifteen separate countries. America was now seen as the winner of the Cold War and the sole remaining superpower by friend and foe alike. Ironically, a communist regime that has remained firmly in power since the end of the Cold War is the one in Vietnam against which the United States fought for so many years. This, however, has not prevented Washington and Hanoi from developing and maintaining close, friendly relations for well over a decade now.

This experience raises an intriguing possibility: if the United States could lose the war in Vietnam but go on to become the acknowledged winner of the Cold War less than two decades later, could it also lose the war in either Afghanistan or Iraq (or even both) and yet go on to win the War on Terror? Some will argue, of course, that the American withdrawal from Vietnam had no connection with the end of the Cold War, or that the Cold War ended in America's favor not because the United States withdrew from Vietnam, but despite its having done so. They would point to the differences between the foreign and defense policies of the Nixon, Ford, and Carter administrations on the one hand and those of the Reagan administration on the other as explaining how the United States could lose the Vietnam War and yet win the overall Cold War. According to this argument, an American withdrawal from Iraq, Afghanistan, or both by the Obama administration will definitely not lead to America winning the War on Terror. To do this, the United States will have to adopt a tougher policy akin to the Reagan administration's.

Although this argument will appeal to many, its logic is flawed. There is a direct connection between America's withdrawal from Vietnam, Cambodia, and Laos and how the Cold War subsequently ended: the American withdrawal from Indochina unleashed or exacerbated forces that directly contributed to Soviet overexpansion in the Third World, the decline of Soviet power and influence, and the end of the Cold War. These forces were the projection of an exaggerated image of American weakness, unrealistic expectations on the part of the USSR and its allies about their own strength and likelihood of prevailing in the Cold War, and divisions within the Marxist camp. Although not foreseen or intended at the time, the Nixon administration's withdrawal from Indochina led to subsequent Soviet overexpansion, which provided the opportunity for the Reagan administration to pursue policies that took advantage of Moscow's predicament.

Could something like this happen again? Although it may seem counterintuitive, an American withdrawal from Iraq and Afghanistan could do more to undermine Islamic radicals and strengthen the ability of America and its allies to deal with them than if the United States remains bogged down militarily in war efforts that it cannot win or can only "win" at an unacceptably high cost.

Beyond Iraq
and Afghanistan

▼ ▼ ▼

Regional and Local Conflicts in the War on Terror

One way that America and its allies could weaken the appeal of Islamic radicalism would be through resolving the various local and regional conflicts that are linked to the overall War on Terror. The resolution of a particular conflict would reduce the motivation of those for whom that conflict is the most salient to join or support radical Islamic groups. If, for example, the Kashmir dispute could be resolved, a few Pakistanis might still take up arms for the Palestinian, Chechen, or some other cause, but probably not the majority for whom Kashmir was their primary grievance. Similarly, most Palestinians are primarily concerned about the Israel-Palestine issue, and most Chechens are primarily concerned about the Chechen issue. Resolving the component conflicts in the overall War on Terror, then, would reduce the recruitment base for groups like Al Qaeda that have sought to make them part of a global conflict.

Further, resolving any one conflict could have a positive effect on some other conflicts. An Israeli-Palestinian peace settlement, for example, not only would benefit the local parties but also could help the United States improve its relations with the Muslim world as a whole. Radical Islamists who reject an agreement accepted by the majority of Palestinians and Muslims elsewhere could well find themselves marginalized. Similarly, peacefully resolving the India-Pakistani conflict over Kashmir not only would end Pakistani assistance to radical Muslim groups targeting India (indeed, this would have to happen in order to resolve this conflict) but also could end Pakistani support for the Taliban, thus facilitating a resolution to the conflict in Afghanistan. Genuine peaceful reconciliation in Iraq would reduce the incentive for Sunni Arabs there to ally with Al Qaeda in Iraq and for Shi'a Arabs to depend on Iran. Resolving the Yemeni government's differences with its many other internal opponents would result in more resources being available to combat Al Qaeda in the Arabian Peninsula (whose strength in Yemen is partially due to the Yemeni government's preoccupation with other domestic threats). The list could go on, but the point should already be clear: resolving the individual conflicts that are linked to the War on Terror will reduce the incentive for those involved in conflicts that are resolved to join or support radical Islamic movements.

While this approach would undoubtedly be the best way to defuse the War on Terror, it has so far proven to be exceptionally difficult—even futile—in some cases. If resolving all—or, indeed, any—of the individual conflicts linked to the War on Terror were simple, this would already have been accomplished. And if this could have been accomplished in enough cases, what has become the all-consuming War on Terror either may have been a much smaller scale affair or may not have occurred at all.

The intractability of local and regional conflicts is not something new. There were also many such conflicts during the Cold War. Indeed, the pervasiveness of the Soviet-American dimension in virtually all of the world's conflicts was so great that their local roots and causes were often overlooked. Thus, when Soviet-American relations dramatically improved at the very end of the Cold War, hope emerged that many of the Third World's seemingly intractable conflicts could be resolved; however, many of them could not.

A personal anecdote illustrates just how intractable some of these conflicts can be. The United States Institute of Peace commissioned me to organize a series of seminars in 1989–90 on the opportunities for and obstacles to Soviet-American conflict resolution in the Third World. In 1991, the papers for this project were published in a book I edited entitled *Soviet-American Conflict Resolution in the Third World*. The book's chapters discussed several conflicts (or conflict-prone situations): security in Asia and the Pacific, an Arab-Israeli peace settlement, Afghanistan, Southern Africa, the Horn of Africa, and Cambodia. In the introduction, I noted that while the authors did not share common views on several issues, there was "general agreement among them on two points: (1) Soviet-American agreement that regional conflicts should be resolved is not sufficient to bring about resolution; and (2) because each regional conflict is unique, successful methods for fully or partially resolving one conflict will not necessarily work for others."

What is interesting about this book now is not what any of the contributors wrote in it over twenty years ago, but to observe what became of the six cases that were studied. Four of these cases are still not resolved. With North Korea issuing nuclear threats and China having grown more assertive, tension in the Asia Pacific region has only increased. An overall Arab-Israeli peace settlement still has not been achieved and does not appear likely any time soon. Afghanistan is still in the midst of a war. And the Horn of Africa (which includes Somalia, Ethiopia, Eritrea, and Sudan) is wracked by chronic conflict. By contrast, conflict resolution did occur in South Africa, Namibia, and Angola, but the fighting in Angola continued from the end of the Cold War until 2002. In addition, conflict resolution in Cambodia was reasonably successful, although implementation of the 1991 Paris Peace Accords required direct United Nations administration of this country in 1992–93.

Comparing the status of these six cases at the end of the Cold War with their status now shows that there is no guarantee that regional and local conflicts can be resolved even after going on for decades. On the other hand, it is sometimes possible to resolve them. Long-standing local and regional conflicts linked to the War on Terror include the Israeli-Palestinian, Iraqi, Afghan,

Yemeni, Somali, Sudanese, Indian-Pakistani, Chechen, Uighur, and Moro ones. Others still may erupt. Past experience suggests that while it may be possible—with great effort—to resolve some of them, resolving all or even most of them is highly unlikely any time soon. And those that are not resolved will continue to provide the best opportunities for Al Qaeda and other radical Islamist movements to gain influence.

In policy terms, then, America and its allies should earnestly work toward resolving regional and local conflicts in order to undercut the appeal of radical Islamic forces in various parts of the Muslim world. The death of bin Laden has not eliminated the need to pursue strategies designed to counter Islamic revolutionary movements and regimes that remain strong or are growing stronger in those parts of the Muslim world where regional and local conflicts persist. I cannot discuss how each and every one of its component conflicts and other problems could or should be addressed in order to reduce the scope and intensity of the overall War on Terror. What I will do instead is examine four especially important regional conflict situations—Israel-Palestine, Iran, Yemen, and Pakistan—in order to see what opportunities and obstacles exist for defusing them as well as decoupling them from the larger War on Terror.

▼ ▼ ▼

The Israeli-Palestinian Conflict

The Israeli-Palestinian conflict's relationship to the War on Terror is unique in that it is of intense concern not just to the immediate parties involved but to so many others as well. On the one hand, American public opinion—as well as the U.S. government—has strongly supported Israel throughout its existence, especially since the 1967 Arab-Israeli War. On the other hand, Arabs and Muslims in general feel deeply aggrieved over the plight of the Palestinians and outraged over American support for Israel. Al Qaeda and other radical Islamist groups have sought to heighten and exploit these feelings in order to secure funding, recruits, and sympathy from Arabs and other Muslims. The Israeli-Palestinian conflict, in short, serves as a *cause célèbre* for Al Qaeda and other radical Islamist movements throughout the Muslim world.

Despite this, the Israeli-Palestinian conflict is one in which Al Qaeda itself appears to play very little direct role. Indeed, the Israeli-Palestinian conflict has been going on since well before Al Qaeda came into existence. Two other movements hold sway among the Palestinians in the Israeli-occupied territories: secular nationalist Fatah in the West Bank and Islamic radical Hamas in Gaza. Al Qaeda has denounced Hamas for "playing by the rules of the West" and participating in elections (even though Hamas won them in 2006). Al Qaeda has also criticized Hamas for its links with Shi'a Iran and Hezbollah, as well as secular Syria (Paz 2010, 188–90).

While the United States has strongly supported Israel for decades, it has also sought to build and maintain good relations with Arab and Muslim countries. Recognizing that U.S. support for Israel is unpopular with these governments—and even more so with their citizens—the United States has long sought a resolution to the Israeli-Palestinian conflict. The U.S. approach to doing so has been to try to broker a negotiated settlement acceptable to both sides. Many Palestinians (and their supporters), however, object to this approach since they see Israel as stronger than the Palestinians (as a result, in large part, of American support for Israel) and thus in a position to resist Palestinian demands.

After years of calling for (if not seriously threatening) Israel's destruction, PLO/Fatah leader Yasir Arafat agreed to seek a peacefully negotiated two-state solution instead. The Oslo peace process led to the formation of the Palestinian Authority. While this was not the independent state that Palestinians sought, it did result in Israel transferring much administrative control of the occupied territories to Fatah. In 2000, the Clinton administration almost succeeded in helping Israel and Fatah achieve a peace agreement resulting in an independent Palestinian state; however, the two sides were unable to overcome all their differences, and so the hoped-for settlement was not reached (Telhami 2001).

In subsequent years, the secular nationalist Fatah lost support among Palestinians to its radical Islamist rival, Hamas. Factors that contributed to this include (1) Fatah's inability to achieve Palestinian aspirations for independence through either violent or peaceful means, (2) the incompetence and corruption of the Fatah-dominated Palestinian Authority, and (3) Hamas's growing ability to deliver social services more effectively and efficiently than the Palestinian Authority. Given these conditions, it is not surprising that Hamas won the 2006 Palestinian parliamentary elections.

Hamas is a Sunni Islamist group. It does not seek a two-state solution, calling instead for the destruction of Israel and the creation of a single, Palestinian state. In addition to opposing Israel, it is engaged in a long-drawn-out power struggle with Fatah. While Fatah still controls (in conjunction with Israel) the West Bank, Hamas was able to seize control over the Gaza Strip after Israel unilaterally withdrew from the latter in 2005.

The Mideast Quartet (the ongoing diplomatic effort aimed at bringing about Arab-Israeli peace being conducted by the United States, European Union, United Nations, and Russia) responded to the Hamas electoral victory by offering to work with Hamas if it met three conditions: renounce violence, recognize Israel, and abide by existing Mideast peace agreements. Hamas rejected all three conditions; its spokesman stated, "The Quartet should have demanded an end to [Israeli] occupation and aggression, not demanded that the victim should recognize the occupation and stand handcuffed in the face of the aggression" (La Guardia and Rennie 2006).

Hamas has maintained this uncompromising position ever since. This has enabled it to project a more positive image to Palestinians, Arabs, and Muslims in general than the compromising (and, in the eyes of many, compromised) Fatah. In addition, Hamas also appears to be more successful than Fatah, in that it has gained and retained control of Gaza in defiance of both Israel and Fatah itself. Fatah, by contrast, appears to retain control of just those parts of the West Bank that Israel allows it too.

Hamas pursues this policy not just because this allows it to look more "principled" than Fatah or even because this is its preference. The Hamas leadership believes that Fatah's willingness to lay down arms and negotiate a settlement is what ultimately led to Hamas's success. Hamas fears that if it too forswore violence, as the Quartet insists, there is no guarantee that it would be any more successful in negotiating an agreement with Israel that the Palestinian population would accept. Even attempting this would leave the door open for a rival Islamist group to do to Hamas what Hamas did to Fatah. One such potential rival already exists: Islamic Jihad (Zaboun 2010). And just as Al Qaeda affiliates (such as Al Qaeda in the Arabian Peninsula, Al Qaeda in

Iraq, and Al Qaeda in the Islamic Maghreb) have arisen elsewhere, an Al Qaeda in Palestine might arise to challenge Hamas if it seeks to compromise with Israel but is unable to wrest concessions from it. Of course, more radical Islamist movements may gain strength in relation to Hamas even if the latter remains committed to its uncompromising position but fails thereby to achieve positive results for the Palestinian people.

Whether they realize it or not (and, unfortunately, some do not), all the current major players in the Israeli-Palestinian conflict—Israel, America and its allies, Fatah, and even Hamas—have an interest in achieving a negotiated settlement acceptable to both Israelis and Palestinians. Their failure to achieve this risks the Israeli-Palestinian conflict becoming much more deeply enmeshed in the War on Terror—an outcome that would undoubtedly benefit Al Qaeda and its affiliates.

▼ ▼ ▼

Iran

Hostility between Iran and America as well as several of its allies (especially Israel) is something that began long before the War on Terror. Shortly after the success of the 1979 Islamic Revolution, Iran sought to export its brand of revolution through supporting Shi'a radicals in the Arab Gulf states as well as in Lebanon and (after Iraq attacked it in 1980) by attempting to oust Saddam Hussein and replace his secular Arab nationalist regime with an Islamic revolutionary one. The Iranian revolutionaries never succeeded in installing a Shi'a radical regime anywhere else; however, they have continued to provide varying degrees of support to Islamic radical forces, including Hezbollah in Lebanon, Hamas in the Israeli-occupied Arab territories, and the Sunni radical regime that rose to power in Sudan in 1989.

In addition to this revolutionary, ideological aspect of Iranian foreign policy, the Islamic Republic has also displayed a pragmatic, realpolitik aspect—especially after the death of Ayatollah Khomeini in 1989, when Tehran had to face the challenges posed by the collapse of the Soviet Union. In the fierce conflict that emerged between Orthodox Christian Armenia and Shi'a Azerbaijan, Iran favored the former. Tehran also worked with

Moscow to resolve the 1992–97 Tajik civil war on terms more favorable to the ex-Communists backed by Moscow and not the "democratic Islamic" opposition. Tehran also worked with Moscow from the time the Taliban seized Kabul in 1996 until after 9/11 in supporting the Northern Alliance's efforts to prevent the Taliban from taking over all of Afghanistan. As Stephen J. Hadley (who was deputy national security adviser during President George W. Bush's first term and national security adviser during his second) acknowledged, Tehran even cooperated with Washington in the initial stages of the U.S.-led intervention in Afghanistan in late 2001 (2010, 142–43). Iran is also a major petroleum exporter; just as before the 1979 Revolution, it has been willing to sell oil to almost any country. (The United States, of course, does not import Iranian oil, but this is due to U.S.—not Iranian—government regulations.)

Ayatollah Khomeini's ambition was that the Iranian Revolution would spark an Islamic revolutionary wave that would spread across the entire Muslim world and even beyond. In his vision, Iran would be at the center of this wave (Walt 1996, 212–16). But however much Sunni radicals in other countries may have been inspired by the Iranian Revolution to attempt Islamic revolution themselves elsewhere, it soon became clear that they did not acknowledge the Iranian ayatollahs or Iran as having any authority over them (Ayubi 1991, 152–55; Haykel 2010). With the rise of the Taliban in the 1990s in neighboring Afghanistan, it became evident that radical Sunni Islamists could be not only anti-Western but also anti-Shi'a and anti-Iranian. Indeed, the Taliban (and later Al Qaeda) espoused an Islamic revolutionary ideology that competed with Tehran's. Further, the spread of this competing Sunni radical Islamic revolutionary ideology not only would challenge Iran's claim to lead the transnational Islamic revolutionary movement but could even threaten Iran itself if the Sunni radicals acted on their anti-Shi'a pronouncements.

Despite the anti-Iranian and anti-Shi'a statements and even actions of the Sunni radicals, Iran has clearly not yet felt threatened enough by them to ask the United States for help against their common foe. In fact, since Mahmoud Ahmadinejad became president of Iran in 2005, Iranian foreign policy has been much more belligerent toward the United States and Israel than under the previous president, Mohammed Khatami.

Under Ahmadinejad, Iran has defied not just America but also the UN Security Council on the nuclear issue (Tehran claims to be working on an exclusively peaceful nuclear program, while the United States and many others fear that it is seeking to acquire nuclear weapons). As mentioned previously, Iran has been supporting (to varying degrees) assorted radical groups in Iraq, Hamas, Hezbollah, and even the Taliban after the United States intervened in Afghanistan (Brandenburg 2010; Eisenstadt 2010; Hokayem 2010; Nader and Laha 2011). Some claim that Tehran is also supporting the Houthis (a Shi'a opposition group in Yemen), but it does not appear to be actually doing so (Winter 2011). Ahmadinejad and Venezuela's "Bolivarian socialist" leader, Hugo Chavez, have also declared great plans to work together in order to defy the United States. Yet at the same time, Ahmadinejad has continued the pragmatic aspect of Iranian foreign policy through cooperating in various ways with other countries, including Russia, China, and many more (including some in the West). Indeed, while many governments have nominally agreed to the U.S. government's call for economic sanctions against Iran over the nuclear issue, corporations in many of them continue to do business with Iran. Finally, and most curiously, Hamid Karzai—the president of the U.S.-backed government in Afghanistan—has admitted that his office receives "bags of money" from Tehran (Arnoldy 2010).

Iran's actions, then, are confusing. It supports Shi'a radicals and even some Sunni radicals elsewhere, but it also works with and even supports some of America's allies. In Iraq and Afghanistan, Tehran supports groups that oppose each other. What is the Iranian government attempting to accomplish through such a policy?

One possibility is that instead of one integrated foreign policy, Tehran may be pursuing different foreign policies toward different countries, or even different groups within a specific country. Perhaps this is the result of a pragmatic effort to work with whoever is willing to work with Tehran. Or perhaps the pursuit of divergent foreign policies is the result of infighting among various interest groups within the Islamic Republic (if so, Iran would not be the only country to experience this phenomenon). But if there is an overall coherence to Iranian foreign policy, and Tehran *deliberately* pursues contradictory aims and supports opposing parties, then two overarching explanations are possible.

The first explanation is that Tehran is pursuing an extraordinarily Machiavellian policy that aims to win over and control not only the region's various radical Islamic groups but also Tehran's ideological antagonists and America's Muslim allies in the region (especially in Afghanistan and Iraq) through aiding them all—with the ultimate aim of displacing the United States as the predominant great power in the Middle East.

The second explanation is that Tehran is pursuing a far more defensive objective. Its support for Hamas and Hezbollah in particular is aimed at competing with Al Qaeda and other radical Sunni movements in projecting a "positive" revolutionary image of Iran to the Arab world in particular. The message Iran is attempting to convey is, "Since Iran supports the 'just cause' of both Hamas and Hezbollah, Sunni radicals should not attack Iran or Iranian interests—and Sunni Arabs should not support those groups that do." At the same time, Iran is working with or supporting its ideological opponents—and even some U.S. allies—in order to give them an incentive not to undertake or support actions harmful to Tehran.

Which of these explanations is correct? The answer to this question will become much clearer as the United States withdraws from Iraq and Afghanistan. After the U.S. departure from Iraq, will the various Shi'a groups there be grateful to Iran for how much it helped each of them? Or will each be resentful that Tehran didn't support it even more, and that Tehran supported its rivals as well? After the United States leaves Afghanistan, will the Taliban be grateful to Iran for its recent support? Or will the Taliban revert to its pre-9/11 policy of targeting Iran and Iranian interests—this time with the aid of the arms, money, or whatever else it recently received from Tehran? And if Iran does indeed find itself increasingly at odds with various Islamic radical actors, will Hamas and Hezbollah be willing or able to help Iran against them?

The answers to these questions are not at all clear, even to Tehran. This is reminiscent of the situation that China was in during the late 1960s and early 1970s. While the United States was heavily involved in Indochina, Beijing had hostile relations both with Washington (its ideological foe) and with Moscow (its erstwhile ideological ally). China appears to have genuinely feared both. But as it became clear that the United States would withdraw from Indochina (and then actually did so), Beijing came to regard Washington not only as less of a threat but also as a potential ally against Moscow.

Just as the U.S. withdrawal from Indochina intensified Sino-Soviet competition, the U.S. withdrawal from Iraq and Afghanistan may well serve to intensify competition between Iran on the one hand and Al Qaeda, the Taliban, other Sunni radical groups, and perhaps even some Shi'a radical groups on the other. A U.S. withdrawal from these two countries, which will make the United States appear weak, will thus encourage various radical Islamic actors to focus more on their internecine struggles and the competition for leadership of the transnational Islamic radical movement. Such actions, of course, could contribute to their undoing.

▼ ▼ ▼

Yemen

Yemen has witnessed many conflicts since the early 1960s. Currently, there is conflict taking place between the Saleh regime and the Houthi rebels in the north. There is also tension between the Saleh regime and southern secessionists. As frequent press reports note, Al Qaeda in the Arabian Peninsula (AQAP) is also active in Yemen. And in early 2011, a democratic opposition to the Saleh regime emerged similar to those that rose up in Tunisia, Egypt, Libya, Bahrain, and Syria.

The United States has become primarily concerned about Yemen because of the Al Qaeda presence there and has sought Yemeni government cooperation in targeting AQAP. The Yemeni government, though, has been more concerned about the Houthis, the southern secessionists, and—most recently—the democratic opposition, which pose a greater threat to it than AQAP does. Indeed, although Yemen has received assistance from the United States for the fight against AQAP, the Yemeni government has also turned to radical Sunnis in the fight against southern secessionists in the 1994 civil war and against the Houthis more recently (Boucek 2010, 12–17).

Yemen is not the first case where a government and an external power supporting it have pursued contradictory aims. Indeed, this is not the first time it has happened in Yemen.

In this conflict, as in so many others, the external power is mainly concerned about the global or regional conflict it is involved in, whereas the local government is mainly concerned about its local opponents. In his *A History of Modern Yemen*, British anthropologist Paul Dresch described how this is the norm in Yemen: "Contests among people in the same moral system are sometimes all that matters, and states, even empires with their grand pretensions, become pawns in games of local interest. This is something of a theme in Yemen's history. . . . Two brothers at odds may seek help, perhaps, from different governments" (2000, 25).

The problem, then, for any outside power (such as the United States) that seeks to side with one Yemeni party against another is that (1) Yemen is highly complex and difficult for outsiders to understand and (2) the Yemenis regard alliances not as fixed and permanent, but as fluid and temporary. While the U.S. government in particular often sees conflict in "you're either with us or against us" terms, for Yemenis, today's enemies can become tomorrow's friends—and vice versa.

Thus, the United States has been disappointed with the Saleh government's inconsistent cooperation with Washington in the War on Terror. While Sana'a aided American efforts to kill or capture Al Qaeda fighters in Yemen for a couple of years after 9/11, its cooperation with the United States then diminished and the Saleh government moved closer to Sunni radicals in an alliance against its other domestic enemies—especially the Houthis.

Saleh's changing behavior can be understood as an effort to balance the internal and external threats he has faced in a rapidly changing situation. His cooperation with the United States in the aftermath of 9/11 and the seemingly successful (at the time) U.S.-led interventions in Afghanistan and Iraq may have been motivated by a desire to avoid direct U.S. military intervention in Yemen—the possibility of which was then being discussed in the American press. But as America and its allies became increasingly bogged down in Afghanistan and Iraq, the possibility of the

United States intervening in Yemen diminished. Just as importantly, the growing strength of both the Houthi rebellion in the north and the secessionist movement in the south not only led the Saleh government to pay more attention to them but also resulted in its cooperating with Sunni radicals against the Shi'a Houthis in particular. This move was similar to Saleh's alliance with Sunni radicals against the southern secessionists during the 1994 Yemeni civil war (Scahill 2011).

Thus, while the United States sees Sunni radicals as its primary opponent in Yemen and other countries, Saleh was willing to ally with Sunni radicals against others whom he viewed as even more threatening. In mid-2009, however, American press reports indicated that Saleh had renewed his cooperation with the United States against AQAP. In his *Washington Post* column of January 28, 2010, David Ignatius wrote, "The breakthrough came last July, when Yemeni President Ali Abdullah Saleh decided that his regime was threatened. It was his fight, in other words, not just ours. 'We had an embrace in July, literally and figuratively,' says Gen. David Petraeus, the Centcom commander who has been the U.S. point man with Yemen."

If Saleh did indeed come to regard Al Qaeda in the Arabian Peninsula as more of a threat than he did previously, then this would certainly explain his renewed cooperation with the United States against it. There could, however, be another explanation for his behavior: seeing that the Obama administration was especially concerned about AQAP and desirous of obtaining American resources in order to fight against his other opponents, Saleh had a strong incentive to make a show of cooperating with the United States against AQAP.

Which explanation is correct? If the Yemeni government's cooperation with Washington against AQAP continued indefinitely, this would support the former explanation. But if, as before, the Yemeni government's cooperation with the United States waned and a degree of tolerance for AQAP in Sana'a reemerged, this would support the latter explanation.

It must be noted that Yemen's complicated political dynamics not only constrain the United States and other external actors but also Al Qaeda. Members of AQAP are protected by various tribes at odds with Sana'a in remote areas of Yemen that the government does not control (Phillips 2010, 80–81). As a result of force, persuasion, or both, the leaders of these tribes could reach an accommodation with Sana'a that results in their expelling or even turning over the AQAP fighters they have hosted. Further, the willingness of various tribes to host AQAP may depend on their shaykhs (tribal leaders) believing that AQAP is weak in relation to, dependent on, and hence not threatening to the tribes. If they see AQAP growing strong enough to threaten the authority of the tribal shaykhs, the latter may quickly turn against it. According to one press report, some of the southern tribes have already done so ("South Yemen Tribes Turn against Qaeda Allies" 2011). Just as the Saleh government has not always been a reliable partner as far as Washington is concerned, AQAP cannot depend on the Yemeni tribes protecting them to remain reliable partners either.

Yemen's internal conflicts and the broader War on Terror are connected but separate. Just as resolving Yemen's internal conflicts will not bring about an end to the War on Terror, resolving the War on Terror will not bring about an end to Yemen's internal conflicts. Indeed, even if—by some miracle—the War on Terror came to an end in a manner advantageous to the West like the Cold War did in 1989–91, Yemen's various internal antagonists can be expected to seek assistance from opposing sides in other regional or global conflicts that either already exist (such as Saudi Arabia vs. Iran) or may yet emerge (such as China vs. the West).

▼ ▼ ▼

Pakistan

Pakistan's relationship to the War on Terror has been highly ambivalent. On the one hand, Pakistan played a key role in facilitating the U.S.-led intervention in Afghanistan from shortly after 9/11 up to the present. It has permitted the transit of materiel across Pakistani territory to U.S. forces in Afghanistan. Pakistan has also tolerated American missile attacks launched from Afghanistan against Taliban and Al Qaeda targets in Pakistan's lawless border region with that country.

On the other hand, Pakistan has provided safe haven not just for radical Islamist movements targeting its rival, India, but also for the Afghan Taliban and the Haqqani network (allies of the Taliban, but separate from them). Al Qaeda leader Osama bin Laden was hiding (from American, if not from Pakistani, authorities) there for years, and his successor, Ayman Al-Zawahiri, and others are also believed to be residing in Pakistan. Who within and to what extent the Pakistani government has been protecting them is unclear, but it certainly has not helped the U.S. government to locate and capture them. There were also press reports that in early 2010 Pakistan arrested about a dozen Taliban leaders who were amenable to peace talks with the U.S.-backed

Karzai government in Kabul (McGirk 2010). This suggests that Pakistan does not want to see the Afghan conflict resolved but cynically prefers it to continue. U.S.-Pakistani relations became increasingly strained after U.S. forces mounted a raid leading to the death of bin Laden inside Pakistan without seeking prior approval for this mission from the Pakistani government (DeYoung and Witte 2011)—a move that would have probably caused the mission to fail.

What explains this ambivalence is that while the United States and Pakistan have some common goals, their priorities differ markedly. The United States was concerned primarily with the Soviet threat during the Cold War and has been primarily concerned with the threat from Al Qaeda and its Taliban allies since 9/11. Pakistan, by contrast, has been primarily concerned with its struggle with India ever since both became independent from Britain in 1947. The fate of Kashmir—the Muslim-majority region that was divided between India and Pakistan during their first war (1947–48)—has been Pakistan's principal concern, but it also has many others, including which of the two rivals will have predominant influence in Afghanistan.

Pakistan has also been vitally concerned with the preservation of its territorial integrity. The country is an agglomeration of ethnicities with little in common except adherence to Islam. In the early 1970s, the conflict between what was then the two parts of the country—West Pakistan and East Pakistan—was essentially one about which ethnicity would dominate the country. Indian intervention in that war allowed what was East Pakistan to secede and become Bangladesh. Since then, the Pakistani military and security services have increasingly emphasized Pakistan's Islamic identity to keep the otherwise disparate ethnic groups of what remained of Pakistan together. But one group has been predominant in the Pakistani military and security services, and hence in the government, ever since independence: the Punjabis (Lieven 2011).

Kashmir provides a rallying point for all Pakistanis who believe that Muslims there should also be able to live in overwhelmingly Muslim Pakistan. But Kashmir has also posed a problem for the Pakistani government and military. Pakistan has been able neither to seize it from India nor to persuade India to give it up. But while it has no real hope of acquiring Indian-held Kashmir, no Pakistani government can afford to acknowledge this or relinquish Pakistan's claim to Kashmir. Doing so not only would be hugely unpopular inside Pakistan but also might encourage other ethnicities (Pushtuns, Sindhis, and Balochis) to push for secession from the Punjabi-dominated state.

During the period of their Cold War alliance, the differing American and Pakistani priorities were evident in that the United States sought Pakistan as an ally against the USSR while Pakistan sought the United States as an ally against India. The height of Pakistani-American cooperation occurred during the Soviet occupation of Afghanistan, when the United States, Pakistan, and many others backed the Afghan mujahideen who were resisting the Soviets. Even then, however, Pakistan favored the Islamist Afghan mujahideen groups over more nationalist groups. Islamabad believed that it would have more influence over the former (Weinbaum 1991).

After the Soviet withdrawal from Afghanistan in 1988–89, American concern about Afghanistan and South Asia in general diminished. Pakistan, however, remained focused on its rivalry with India. During the 1990s, Pakistan supported the rise of the Taliban for several reasons: to restore order in what had become a chaotic country, to promote an Islamist ally that would sympathize with Pakistan over Kashmir and thus resist Indian influence, to establish a secure road network across Afghanistan to link Pakistan with newly independent Central Asia (thus benefiting the politically powerful Pakistani trucking industry), and even to extend Pakistani influence across Afghanistan into Central Asia. The Pakistani military and security services also believed that having an ally in Afghanistan would give Pakistan "strategic depth" in any future confrontation with India (though precisely what this meant and how it would work were ill-defined and poorly thought out) (Shafi 2010).

With Pakistani help, the Taliban was able to seize control of most of Afghanistan in 1996. The Taliban, however, proved to be an extremely difficult ally for Pakistan. The Taliban provided safe haven to several radical Islamist groups, including Al Qaeda. After Al Qaeda launched the 9/11 attacks and it became clear that the United States would intervene militarily in Afghanistan in retaliation, the Bush administration forced Pakistan to choose between siding with the United States and siding with the Taliban. Pakistan formally chose to side with the United States not because of a genuine Pakistani change of heart regarding the Taliban, but because of the fear that the United States would side with India against Pakistan if it did not; Islamabad hoped that siding with (or appearing to side with) the United States against the Taliban would strengthen Pakistan in relation to India. Anticipating that the United States would not remain in Afghanistan and that the Taliban, and perhaps even Al Qaeda, might prove useful to it, Pakistan tolerated and even supported their presence on its territory in the region bordering Afghanistan (Gul 2010, 147–86; Woodward 2010, 4; Bergen 2011, 247–65).

Indeed, it would be difficult for Pakistan to do otherwise. Pakistan has long supported radical Islamist groups that are primarily concerned with Kashmir and India. How could it draw a distinction between these "good" Muslim radicals and "bad" Taliban ones, especially when Pakistani public opinion views both favorably? But at the same time, the Pakistani government has not wanted to alienate the United States either (or at least not alienate it too much). Thus, Pakistani policy since 9/11 has been a confusing mixture of supporting, sheltering, and tolerating the Taliban and Al Qaeda to some extent, but also supporting U.S. actions against them at the same time.

Not surprisingly, the U.S. government has grown increasingly frustrated with Pakistan because its support for the Taliban has hurt American military efforts in Afghanistan. But many Pakistani—especially Pushtun—Islamists condemn the Pakistani government for cooperating with the United States at all. Indeed, a Pakistani Taliban has arisen—mainly among Pakistan's Pushtun population—that has fought against Pakistani government forces (Pape and Feldman 2010, 143–44). At this point, a Pakistani government decision to turn against these radical Islamist forces—or just end its support for them—might result in accelerating a genuine homegrown radical threat to the Pakistani government itself.

Despite this, the Pakistani leadership has—characteristically—remained focused on its rivalry with India. With the United States and NATO having announced that they will withdraw from Afghanistan between mid-2011 and the end of 2014, Pakistan seems more worried than ever that the Karzai government will ally with India to the detriment of Pakistan. And so, Pakistan has continued to support the hard-line Afghan Taliban. The irony of its doing this, of course, is that if the Taliban returns to power in Afghanistan with Pakistan's help, the Taliban is hardly likely to be more amenable to Pakistani influence since it will then require less support from Islamabad—just as occurred during the 1990s. Indeed, if the Afghan Taliban decides to help its Pushtun brethren across the border in Pakistan, the Pakistani government may find itself faced with its own very serious Islamist insurgency—and an unsympathetic international community as a result of the policies Pakistan has pursued up to now.

▼ ▼ ▼

═══════════════════
═══════════════════

Decoupling Regional and Local Conflicts from the War on Terror

The linkage of four specific conflict situations to the War on Terror—Israel-Palestine, Iran, Yemen, and Pakistan—was discussed in the four previous chapters. But after failing to do so up to the present, can America and its allies now hope to somehow become successful in decoupling any of these from the War on Terror, or at least reducing their linkage to it?

It seems safe to assume that U.S. policies that have not succeeded in the past are not likely to succeed in the future either. Resolving the problems posed by Israel-Palestine, Iran, Yemen, and Pakistan—and reducing their linkage to the War on Terror—will thus require new approaches. Some possibilities are examined below.

Israel-Palestine

America and its allies have been trying unsuccessfully for decades to broker a negotiated settlement to the Israeli-Palestinian dispute. Especially after Hamas took over Gaza following Israel's unilateral withdrawal from there, Israel has sought a settlement that would maintain its security and allow Jewish settlers to remain in the West Bank. Additionally, it wants to retain control of the movement of people and goods in and out of Gaza. These conditions, however, are unacceptable to Palestinians, who regard settling for a Palestinian state in the West Bank and Gaza—and not all of Palestine—as a tremendous (indeed, for Hamas, as too great a) concession to Israel. What makes compromise especially difficult is that the actual geography that encompasses the Israeli-Palestinian conflict is extremely small, and each side is convinced not only of the righteousness of its position but also that making concessions will put its own survival at risk. Given these circumstances, it is hardly surprising that any attempt by outside parties to broker a negotiated settlement has not succeeded.

What may be needed to break this impasse is a settlement similar to those achieved in Bosnia and Kosovo, which involved deploying multinational forces. Specifically, such a settlement should include the following elements: the complete withdrawal of Israeli security forces from the West Bank, an end to Israeli control over the movement of people and goods between the West Bank and Gaza on the one hand and countries besides Israel on the other (including an end to the Israeli naval blockade of Gaza), the deployment of peacekeeping forces from each of the five permanent members of the UN Security Council (and possibly other countries) under a unified command primarily along the borders that the West Bank and Gaza share with Israel, a cease-fire between Israel and the Palestinian governing authorities in the West Bank and Gaza, enforcement of the cease-fire by the multinational peacekeeping forces (not Israeli or Palestinian forces), international recognition of both an elected Palestinian government and Israel, the withdrawal of all Israeli settlers from the West Bank in exchange for the Palestinians foreswearing any "right of return" to Israel, and the establishment of normal trade relations between Israel and Palestine.

Achieving a settlement such as this, of course, is highly doubtful. Yet while neither side would achieve its maximal goals, it would be more advantageous to both sides than the continuation of the present, volatile situation. The Palestinians would undoubtedly prefer to have no outside forces present in their territory, but a

UN Security Council–sponsored peacekeeping force presence would surely be preferable to continued Israeli occupation. Similarly, Israel would benefit from a settlement that would bring about an end to the many burdensome costs—human, financial, and diplomatic—it incurs through its continued occupation of the West Bank and isolation of the Gaza Strip, as well as from the enhanced international acceptance of Israel that agreeing to such a settlement would offer and which Israel craves. But most importantly, if a settlement defusing the Israeli-Palestinian conflict could be achieved, this would eliminate the Palestinian cause as a recruiting tool for Al Qaeda and other jihadists and thus finally decouple the Israeli-Palestinian conflict from the War on Terror.

Iran

America and many of its allies have unsuccessfully sought for many years to constrain Iran's nuclear program (in order to prevent Tehran from acquiring nuclear weapons) and to halt its support for radical Islamist movements in other countries. The United States in particular has attempted to achieve these goals through a policy of containment and increased economic sanctions. Although these policies have not succeeded in changing Iran's behavior, the United States and others continue to pursue them—partly because attempts to engage Tehran (either by others or, on rare occasion, by the United States itself) have also failed.

President Obama attempted to improve relations with Tehran shortly after he came into office at the beginning of 2009. But when this did not succeed, the administration worked to intensify the sanctions regime against Iran. Yet while the Obama administration has certainly gained more cooperation from other countries in imposing sanctions against Iran than the Bush administration did, no progress has yet been made in altering Iran's behavior either on the nuclear or any other issue. Despite this, the Obama administration appears likely to continue trying to further intensify sanctions against Iran.

As was argued earlier, just as the U.S. withdrawal from Indochina intensified competition between the Chinese and the

Soviets, a U.S. withdrawal from Iraq may drive competition between Iran and various Arab Sunni radical groups. If Iran's rivalry
with these radical Sunnis becomes strong enough that Tehran
feels increasingly threatened by them, it may well seek to down-
play its rivalry with the United States—just as both China and
the USSR did after their rivalry heated up during the Cold War.
Iran is clearly not anywhere near this point yet, but Washington
ought to be on the alert for this possibility arising despite current
Iranian-American differences over the nuclear issue and Tehran's
support for Hezbollah, Hamas, and similar groups. The U.S.
government should be aware of the possibility that if Iran feels
sufficiently threatened by Sunni radicals to turn to Washington
for help, then it might well meet American demands on these
other issues.

Indeed, single-mindedly pressing Iran on the nuclear issue
with increased sanctions and other forms of containment may
only serve to delay Iranian recognition that the United States is
not its primary opponent and that Tehran could turn to Washington in the face of a common radical Sunni threat. Additionally, Washington should not forget (as the Iranians have certainly
not forgotten) that China's possession of nuclear weapons and
differences with the United States over Taiwan did not stand in
the way of Sino-American cooperation against the common Soviet threat that began in the early 1970s. Even Iranian possession
of nuclear weapons, then, is not necessarily an obstacle to Iranian-
American cooperation.

Yemen

Even if the Israeli-Palestinian, Iraqi, Afghan, and Iranian problems were to be successfully resolved, Yemen—afflicted as it is
with internal conflict, poverty, illiteracy, and a weak government—
would remain a serious concern. With its large, growing population and its proximity to Saudi Arabia and other petroleum-
producing Gulf countries, Yemen's problems could easily spill
over and negatively affect both its neighbors and all who depend
on them for oil and gas supplies.

What can be done to ameliorate conditions in Yemen, weaken

Al Qaeda in the Arabian Peninsula (AQAP), and decouple Yemen from the War on Terror? One option that the United States should definitely not choose is to intervene militarily in Yemen in response to AQAP's (usually unsuccessful) attacks outside Yemen. Unlike the Houthis, the southern secessionist movement, or the democratic opposition, AQAP really does not have a large following inside Yemen (Phillips 2010, 75). Indeed, many Yemenis describe AQAP as a Saudi opposition movement that was driven out of the Kingdom and has taken advantage of Yemen's internal weakness to find refuge among certain tribes at odds with the government. Instead of fearing U.S. intervention, AQAP would like nothing better than to provoke it because Yemen's rugged terrain would prove as difficult for American forces as Afghanistan's. Foreign intervention would also inflame Yemeni nationalist sentiment, discredit the Yemeni government either for allowing foreign intervention or for being unable to prevent it, and perhaps even result in far more recruits for AQAP than it had been able to attract previously.

America and its allies should instead promote internal Yemeni conflict resolution between the government and its main opponents—the Houthis, the southern secessionists, and (most especially) the democrats. Although the Yemenis have fought among themselves on numerous occasions over the past half century, they have also engaged in some remarkable internal conflict resolution efforts. The 1962 revolution that overthrew North Yemen's king and established a "republic" led to a civil war between republican and monarchist forces that dragged on until 1970; however, the conflict was brought to an end by a conflict resolution process that integrated the royalists (with the exception of the royal family itself) into the republic (Stookey 1978, 251–60). Similarly, the 1990 unification of Marxist South Yemen with non-Marxist North Yemen was the result of an elaborate negotiating process between the two governments that led to a detailed set of agreements over how they would integrate. The latter effort, unfortunately, broke down in 1993, leading to an abortive attempt to reestablish southern independence in 1994, which ultimately led to a reinforced unification on an authoritarian basis (Hudson 1995). The unsatisfactory nature of this outcome eventually resulted in both a revival of the southern secessionist movement and AQAP being especially successful at attracting recruits from among the southerners.

America and its allies should encourage Yemenis to do again what they did before in the realm of conflict resolution. Nor should Washington accept at face value the Saleh government's claims that the Houthis are backed by Iran and that the southern secessionists and AQAP are one and the same. To do so would risk making the same mistake as during the Cold War when authoritarian regimes allied to the United States often branded all their internal opponents as being Marxist in order to undermine American support for democratic reform. But as the United States learned painfully during the Cold War years, vigorous authoritarian rulers can often maintain order for years or even decades, only to lose control and be overthrown when they become old and infirm. By contrast, while a federal democracy in Yemen would undoubtedly be quite messy (just like in Iraq), this form of government could be more effective at preserving unity through granting powerful actors (such as the Houthis, the southern secessionists, and the tribes) both local autonomy and sufficient influence at the national level to give them an interest in preserving a unified Yemen. In addition, accommodating Yemen's democratic opposition could serve to isolate and undercut Al Qaeda elements in Yemen.

Pakistan

Although Pakistan has provided vital support for the U.S.-led intervention in Afghanistan through allowing materiel to transit from its Indian Ocean ports across Pakistani territory into Afghanistan, Islamabad remains primarily focused on its decades-old rivalry with India. Thus, Pakistan has continued to support jihadist groups primarily concerned with "liberating" Indian-controlled Kashmir and to tolerate and even support the Taliban and its allies in order to prevent the growth of Indian influence in Afghanistan. The United States has tried long and hard to persuade Pakistan to abandon this policy of supporting jihadist groups (particularly the Taliban) but has only met with limited success—partly because Pakistan's efforts to crack down on jihadists in the region bordering Afghanistan have met with fierce resistance and have been highly unpopular with the Pakistani public. Furthermore, the American military's logistics are highly dependent on Pakistan, providing Islamabad with sufficient leverage to not cooperate with the United States on this matter. The Obama administration's announcement that American troops would be withdrawn from Afghanistan between mid-2011 and the end of 2014 has only increased (in Islamabad's view) the ability of Pakistan to ignore American demands (Jamal 2011).

Clearly, the United States has failed to decouple Pakistan from the War on Terror. Indeed, the relationship between Pakistan and the War on Terror is fundamentally different from that of any other local or regional conflict linked to it. Possessing a population larger than that of Russia and an arsenal of nuclear weapons, Pakistan is an aspiring great power. Islamabad's policy of protecting or even supporting jihadist groups such as Al Qaeda, the Taliban, and Lashkar-e-Taiba is part and parcel of its ambitions to spread its own influence and limit that of its rival, India. It should not be surprising, then, that American efforts to persuade Pakistan to jettison this policy have failed.

But it is clear that Pakistan's continuing support of these jihadist organizations is highly detrimental to the interests of America, the American-sponsored government in Afghanistan, India, Russia, and many other countries. If the United States cannot persuade Pakistan to change its ways, then it needs to adopt a policy of imposing costs on Pakistan until it abandons these harmful tactics and policies. The United States, of course, is unlikely to adopt such an approach so long as it remains dependent on supply lines through Pakistan to support the large American troop presence in Afghanistan. Once the American troop presence in Afghanistan has been greatly reduced or even eliminated, however, this American dependence on Pakistan will cease, thus allowing the United States far greater freedom to pursue a strategy of containment toward Pakistan if it continues to support the jihadists.

What would a containment strategy directed at Pakistan look like? At minimum, the United States could supply arms to Afghan forces willing to resist the return to power of the Pakistani-backed Taliban. This could be done by way of the recently established Northern Distribution Network (both air and land routes to Afghanistan that run through Russia and Central Asia). Since the governments of Russia and some of the Central Asian republics very much fear that the return of the Taliban to power in Afghanistan will have a highly adverse effect on them, they could well be expected to contribute to such an effort. India might contribute to it too. Fearing that both Pakistan and a Taliban-ruled Afghanistan might support radical Sunni opposition forces inside Iran, even Tehran might join in this containment effort—similarly to how it and Russia both aided the Northern Alliance resisting the Taliban during its rule from 1996 through 2001. Just as the United States, its international partners, and its non-Pushtun allies have encountered fierce resistance in the Pushtun-dominated regions of southern Afghanistan, the Pushtun-dominated Taliban may encounter stiff resistance from non-Pushtun forces in northern Afghanistan backed by the United States and others in opposing the return of the Taliban's misrule, which they well remember.

A more Machiavellian American foreign policy would seek to undercut the relationship between the Pakistani security forces on the one hand and the Pushtuns on the other through taking up the Pushtun nationalist cause. Arguing that the division of the Pushtuns between Afghanistan and Pakistan was the artificial creation of nineteenth-century British imperialism, the United States might propose that the Pushtuns of both southern Afghanistan *and* northern Pakistan be allowed to vote in referendums on whether they wished to secede from the state they are now in and become part of an independent Pushtunistan. Pakistan would virulently oppose any such initiative. American support for it, then, could be expected to result in Pushtun nationalists (including many in the Taliban) seeing Pakistan as their primary opponent, and not the United States. And just as Moscow's enormous nuclear arsenal did not serve to protect the USSR from the rising tide of non-Russian nationalism in the Gorbachev era, Islamabad's much smaller nuclear arsenal will not protect it against Pushtun (and perhaps other non-Punjabi) nationalism. (The non-Pushtuns of northern Afghanistan, of course, will not like this initiative at first either; however, it might be possible to convince them that they would be better off if the Pushtuns did secede since it is unlikely that this group will ever give up in its attempts to regain dominance over Afghanistan within its present borders.)

This may seem like a harsh policy. But since engaging Pakistan for many years has only helped it to aid jihadist forces targeting other countries, containing Pakistan would at least force Islamabad to understand that it faces serious costs for continuing this policy. And unlike current engagement policies, containing Pakistan might hasten the day when Islamabad finally acknowledges that since it can neither force nor persuade India to give up Kashmir, its only hope for a prosperous, stable future is to end all efforts to regain Kashmir (even if it does not give up its claim). Instead, it would be in Pakistan's best interests to pursue friendly relations with its increasingly richer and more powerful Indian neighbor in order to advance its own economic development and build a strong democracy in Pakistan itself. Concerning the status of Muslims in India (whether in Kashmir or elsewhere), Pakistan should limit itself to urging New Delhi to live up to India's own democratic ideals by protecting their rights and assuring them equal opportunity. If Pakistan did this, it not only would decouple itself from the War on Terror but might just make the single most important contribution to ending it.

Conclusion

Even if the United States did adopt the policies proposed here and all of them were successful, the War on Terror still would not end. There are plenty of other regional and local conflicts remaining to feed it, including Chechnya and other Muslim nationalisms in Russia, Uighur nationalism in Xinjiang (China's northwestern province), the Moro rebellion in the southern Philippines (which has actually been going on, more or less, since the late nineteenth century), the clash between Muslims and Buddhists in southern Thailand, Kashmir and the status of Muslims generally in India (even without the Pakistani dimension), Lebanon's seemingly eternal intercommunal clashes, the collapsed state of Somalia, the status of Muslims in Europe, and more. In addition, there is the problem of so many predominantly Muslim countries (including such important ones as Algeria, Saudi Arabia, Iran, the Central Asian republics, and many more) being ruled by authoritarian regimes (whether pro- or anti-American) that do not permit democratic reform or even allow much (if any) democratic opposition, thus driving many of those seeking change into the ranks of seemingly more powerful nondemocratic, radical Islamist opposition movements.

The United States cannot resolve all of these problems. Indeed, it may not be able to resolve any of them, including the four discussed here. The War on Terror, then, is likely to continue. There are, however, new factors and broader contexts affecting it, including how it might be transformed or even end, which will be considered next.

New Factors
and Broader Contexts

▼ ▼ ▼

The Death of Osama bin Laden

On May 2, 2011, the elite U.S. Navy SEAL Team 6 unit killed Al Qaeda leader Osama bin Laden in a raid on his hitherto secret residence in Abbottabad, Pakistan. The most immediate effect of this action was the exacerbation of the already considerable tensions between the United States and Pakistan. For the U.S. government and the American public generally, the discovery of bin Laden in Pakistan—where he had apparently been living for several years—has heightened suspicion that, despite its many denials, the Pakistani military and security establishment not only knew about his presence in their country but also must have facilitated it. For their part, the Pakistani military and security establishment considered the U.S. military raid that killed bin Laden as both embarrassing for revealing that bin Laden was comfortably ensconced in Pakistan and an affront since the United States undertook it without obtaining prior permission from Islamabad—or even informing the Pakistani government about it until after U.S. forces had exited Pakistan. The subsequent revelation that the Navy SEALs were authorized to "return fire" if they were opposed by Pakistani forces (Schmitt, Shanker, and Sanger 2011) was a further indication of just how much the Washington-

Islamabad relationship has deteriorated, as well as how difficult it may be for them to further cooperate with each other.

Bin Laden's death has also affected American public opinion. The capture or killing of the Al Qaeda leader was seen by many Americans as one of the most important aims of the U.S.-led intervention in Afghanistan. A May 2011 *USA Today* / Gallup poll indicated that nearly 60 percent of the American public saw the achievement of this goal as reason for now withdrawing American armed forces from this increasingly unpopular war (Page 2011).

Otherwise, bin Laden's death has principally been noteworthy for its lack of impact. His demise certainly has not ameliorated the War on Terror. Its component conflicts—Afghanistan, Iraq, Yemen, among others—all continue, as does Al Qaeda itself and its various regional affiliates. On the other hand, the death of bin Laden has not exacerbated the War on Terror either. Indeed, consumed by the Arab Spring since its inception in January 2011, the Arab world appears to have barely noticed or cared about bin Laden's death (Sly 2011). The one country where there has been some negative reaction is Pakistan: the Pakistani Taliban vowed revenge for bin Laden's death and launched several terrorist attacks against Pakistani security forces—apparently because they failed to prevent this ("Pakistani Taliban Vow Revenge Attacks on U.S. Targets" 2011).

The Obama administration did run a risk in deciding to kill bin Laden instead of capturing him because in death he could have become even more of an inspiring revolutionary hero than when he was alive, as occurred with Che Guevara after he was killed by Bolivian government forces in 1967. News reports made it clear that the Navy SEALs could have captured bin Laden instead of killing him, but they did not (Gerstein and Negrin 2011). No doubt one consideration in the Obama administration's preference for killing instead of capturing him was that it did not want bin Laden to make a circus of his trial the way Saddam Hussein did after he was captured, even eliciting a degree of sympathy for himself. But whatever the Obama administration's reasoning, bin Laden has so far shown little sign of achieving the sort of eternal revolutionary folk hero status that Guevara did.

What impact—or lack of one—that bin Laden's death may have, of course, is yet to be determined. Much easier to determine is the state of Al Qaeda from the computer files that the Navy SEALs captured when they killed him. From the information that the U.S. government has released about these files, it is clear that while Al Qaeda was still actively plotting attacks against the United States, it was also suffering from numerous problems. These included a lack of money, the loss of many Al Qaeda leaders as a result of American drone attacks killing so many of them, and the penetration of the organization by informants. Even more tellingly, correspondence between bin Laden and his deputy, al-Zawahiri, "express[ed] frustration that the conflict between al-Qaeda and the United States is not more widely perceived among Muslims as the front of a religious war. They also voice[d] concern about how insurgent killings of civilians in Iraq and elsewhere could undermine al-Qaeda's standing among Muslims" (Miller 2011). Further, bin Laden's constantly reminding the regional Al Qaeda affiliates such as AQAP to focus on American targets suggests that regional and local issues are of far greater concern to the affiliates than to Al Qaeda Central. Finally, it must have been a bitter pill for bin Laden to swallow when he found it necessary to warn AQAP in 2010 that "it wasn't the right time" to try to establish an Islamic state in Yemen because this lacked "adequate support" among the Yemeni populace (Miller 2011).

The War on Terror may not be going as well for the United States as Washington would like. What is clear from bin Laden's captured computer files, however, is that it is not going as well for Al Qaeda as its leadership would like either.

▼ ▼ ▼

The Arab Spring

The extraordinary uprisings in the Arab world that began in early 2011 have already achieved extraordinary results: the downfall of Tunisia's, Egypt's, and Libya's long-ruling authoritarian leaders, and the injury of Yemen's. Major opposition activity has also erupted in Bahrain and Syria. In addition, there has been significant unrest in Morocco, Jordan, and Oman. These events are reminiscent of 1989, when a wave of democratization swept through many communist countries. But the 1989 democratic revolutionary wave that arose in both Eastern Europe and China has a cautionary legacy: it succeeded in the former but failed in the latter. It is, of course, not yet clear how successful the current democratic revolutionary wave in the Arab world will be. Whatever the outcome of these uprisings, they will certainly affect the War on Terror. Just how they will do so is difficult to foretell, but once again, an examination of Cold War history can shed light on what their impact might be.

The Cold War involved a confrontation between Western democracy and Marxism-Leninism. In much of the Third World, however, the United States supported authoritarian regimes because democratic forces there were often weak and because Washington feared that if it pushed for the democratization of pro-American authoritarian regimes, the Marxist-Leninists might win the first elections and then destroy democracy. The result would be that a pro-American dictatorship would be replaced by an anti-American one.

Concern about this prospect was so great that the U.S. government often doubted claims by political movements opposed to pro-American dictatorships that they were democratic. On occasion, Washington even worked for the overthrow of democratically elected leaders or governments that it feared were going in "the wrong direction." Some of the most famous (or infamous) examples of this policy were American support for the ouster of Mohammad Mossadeq as prime minister of Iran in 1953 and the overthrow of both the Arbenz government in Guatemala in 1954 and the Allende government in Chile in 1973.

These policies sometimes succeeded in the short run: more reliably pro-American albeit authoritarian regimes were installed or maintained in power. But there was a long-term cost: resentment against the United States arose not just in the country concerned but in many others as well. This allowed Marxist (and other authoritarian revolutionary) movements opposed to pro-American authoritarian regimes to more credibly argue that the United States opposed democratization. Thus, the American policy of supporting pro-American authoritarian regimes because they were seen as more reliable sometimes backfired and resulted in the anti-American authoritarian opposition being better able to seize power than the democratic opposition when these regimes fell.

The United States, however, didn't always support pro-American authoritarian regimes that were losing their grip. Republican administrations, for example, helped bring about successful transitions from pro-American authoritarian regimes to democratic ones in the Philippines in 1986, in South Korea in 1987, and in Chile in 1988–90. Of course, from the Gorbachev era onward, it was less risky for the United States to support democratic transitions in the non-Muslim regions of the world since the rise of pro-Soviet Marxist-Leninists became first a lesser concern and then not a concern at all.

In most of the Muslim world, however, Washington feared that attempts at democratization would lead to the rise of anti-American Islamic fundamentalist regimes. This became a particular concern as a result of the 1979 Iranian revolution. In the Muslim world, then, the older logic still seemed to hold: democratization was something that, however desirable, was just too risky to promote. Furthermore, there didn't appear to be much of a credible democratic opposition in most of these countries anyway. George W. Bush's attempt to move away from this logic, as noted earlier, foundered: the electoral victory of Hamas in 2006 was not the result that the Bush administration had expected when it called for Palestinian parliamentary elections. Further, the Obama administration initially became more committed to the older policy of supporting stability over democracy.

Even when it came to Iran, President Obama gave only tepid and belated support for the extraordinary Green Movement that erupted in the streets of Iranian cities to protest the widely disbelieved Iranian government announcement that Mahmoud Ahmadinejad had won reelection as president by a wide margin in mid-2009. This may have been due to the Obama administration's hope of achieving agreement over the Iranian nuclear issue with Tehran, a calculation that the democratic opposition was doomed to failure anyway, and the mistaken expectation that Iranian hard-liners would be more willing to cooperate on the nuclear issue if Washington did not support their democratic opponents (Katz 2009).

The Arab uprisings of 2011 have posed a serious dilemma for the United States. These movements are genuinely popular. But are they democratic, or are they radical Islamist? Are they pro-American or anti-American? Should the United States remain supportive of the authoritarian regimes (if not the dictators themselves) in long-allied countries for fear that anti-American forces will come to power otherwise? Or should the United States abandon its long-standing authoritarian allies (who may indeed be beyond saving) and support a democratic transition process despite the risk that anti-American forces might come to power through democratic means and then abolish democracy?

One thing is certain: whichever course of action the United States chooses, it cannot avoid risk. Which risk, then, should it run?

Supporting existing authoritarian regimes may appear to be the safer option. Of course, if the United States does this and one or more of these regimes fall anyway, relations with the new regime are not likely to be good for some time. But even if this policy works—that is, the opposition is crushed and the status quo remains intact—the long-term danger is that the United States will be resented as the enemy of democratic change, and the conviction will arise that support for a jihadist revolutionary alternative is the only way to get rid of a hated pro-American regime.

There is no doubt that supporting a democratic transition means accepting certain risks. One risk is that the United States ceases its support for an authoritarian regime, but that regime survives anyway. This will clearly complicate U.S. relations with it. Another is, as mentioned before, that the democratic transition process will lead to the rise of an anti-American authoritarian regime. This scenario should not be dismissed: the risk involved of supporting a democratic transition with this result is real. And yet it is very much in American interests to run this risk and not to adopt the seemingly safer policy of continuing to support a pro-American authoritarian regime that only fosters resentment and a more thoroughgoing anti-American opposition.

For just as the United States cannot be certain what the outcome of a democratic transition process in Arab countries will be, neither can the hard-line Islamic radicals. Indeed, the widespread protests that have erupted throughout the Arab world have caught the radical Islamists off guard. Islamic radicals have played little or no role in Tunisia. Far from orchestrating the demonstrations against Mubarak in Cairo, the Muslim Brotherhood only joined them once they had gotten under way. Al Qaeda in the Arabian Peninsula appears to be playing little role in the popular opposition against the Saleh regime in Yemen (Black 2011), and radical Islamists also seemed to be absent from the opposition movement against Qaddafi in Libya (Pargeter 2011).

Just as the large-scale protests taking place in the Arab world pose a challenge for America and American-backed regimes, they also pose a challenge for hard-line Islamic radicals. If hard-line Islamists attempt to gain control of these popular movements, these movements may well resist them—and even search for allies, such as America, to help them do so. But if the hard-line Islamists do not gain control of these popular movements, they risk being marginalized by them. Instead of leading to the Islamists taking power, then, the democratization process could well result in their failure to do so.

While popular demands for democratization in the Arab world pose challenges for American foreign policy, they also present it with opportunities. If the United States can help the democratization process in the Arab world now, it has an opportunity to establish good relationships with these new governments and to marginalize the radicals. Although it might not come to a complete end, the War on Terror could be diminished markedly in a relatively short period of time. This is an opportunity that the United States cannot afford to forego.

▼ ▼ ▼

The Geopolitical Context

The War on Terror is not taking place in a void. Other geopolitical developments affecting international relations on a global scale are also occurring. Indeed, it is possible that some of these other developments may be more important for international relations in the long term than the War on Terror—however long that may last. Two obvious such possibilities are the rise of China and of India, but there may also be others.

A similar process occurred during the Cold War. While Soviet-American competition was the main event during this era, several other geopolitically important events also occurred: the dismantling of the West European colonial empires; the independence of their former colonies in Asia, the Middle East, Africa, and elsewhere; the emergence of Sino-Soviet hostility followed a few years later by the emergence of Sino-American cooperation; the growth—as well as the growth in importance—of what would become the European Union; and the initiation of what the late Samuel Huntington (1993) referred to as the "third wave" of democratization that began with Spain and Portugal in 1975, crested with the demise of communism in Eastern Europe in 1989, and continued in several other countries afterward. Some of these developments have arguably had a greater impact on present-day international relations than the Cold War did.

The two most significant geopolitical events in the international relations arena that are contemporaneous with the War on Terror era are the rise of China and India as great powers. Other geopolitically important events besides the War on Terror that could have a major impact on international relations are the further development of the European Union; Russia's attempted resurgence; the rise of Brazil, Indonesia, and possibly other powers; and the fate of other, non-Islamist revolutionary enterprises, especially the Bolivarian socialist one led by Hugo Chavez in Latin America and the Maoist one in South Asia. Any of these possibilities, however, could also prove illusory.

The point here is not to try to forecast what geopolitical developments in addition to the War on Terror may or may not occur. The questions that will be addressed instead are as follows: How has the War on Terror (especially the way in which the United States has prosecuted it) affected the larger geopolitical context of international relations? And how have events since 9/11 affected relations among the great powers, as well as the overall balance of power among them?

The entities that are commonly acknowledged as now being or on the cusp of becoming great powers are America, the European Union, Russia, China, and India. Relations among these five are neither completely friendly nor completely hostile. Some of the bilateral relations among them are friendlier (especially between the United States and the European Union), while others are more wary (such as between the United States and Russia and between China and India). Interestingly, one common connection among all five is that even before 9/11 (indeed, long before it in some cases), each of them has had contentious relations with one or more Muslim opponents.

Arab and Muslim opposition to U.S. support for Israel, hostile relations between the United States and Iran since the latter's 1979 revolution, and Osama bin Laden's campaign to expel the United States from the Muslim world, which began when the United States and its allies sent hundreds of thousands of troops to protect Saudi Arabia during the 1990–91 Gulf conflict, are all well known. The European Union—and European governments in general—has been far more sympathetic to the Palestinians, critical of Israel, and more willing to do business with Iran than the United States. Europe, however, has been far more worried than the United States by the prospects of Islamic radicalism in nearby North Africa and, even more, by the growing Muslim communities within Europe itself.

Moscow found itself at war with Western-backed Islamists in Afghanistan during the 1980s. Of even more concern for Moscow is its own internal struggle with one of its Muslim regions—Chechnya—where there have been secessionist efforts ever since the breakup of the USSR in 1991. Islamic radicalism has also spread from Chechnya to other Muslim regions of Russia's North Caucasus in recent years.

Although the unrest in Buddhist Tibet is better known in the West, there has been much fiercer Muslim opposition to Chinese rule just to the northwest in the area that Beijing refers to as Xinjiang. The breakup of the USSR in 1991 and the birth of five independent states in neighboring Central Asia served to spur demands for the independence of this region, which the Muslim Uighurs seeking it refer to as East Turkestan. The mass influx of Han Chinese settlers into this region, however, makes achieving this goal highly unlikely.

Opposition to rule by predominantly Hindu India in the Muslim-majority province of Kashmir is well known. India's long-standing hostile relationship with predominantly Muslim Pakistan over which of them rightfully owns Kashmir is a key element of the ongoing dispute between New Delhi and Islamabad.

Even before 9/11, then, both established great powers and aspiring ones had been fighting against various Muslim opponents. Each of them, however, fought its Muslim opponents with little sympathy or support from the others. Indeed, considerable external aid for the Afghan mujahideen fighting against the Soviet occupation in Afghanistan came not just from the Muslim world but also from the United States and several European countries. The Chechen cause also enjoyed sympathy in the United

States—and even more so in Europe—prior to 9/11. In South Asia, the long-standing U.S. alliance with Pakistan and Soviet alliance with India during the Cold War resulted in the United States and India being at odds during much of this period. Sino-Indian rivalry also resulted in China supporting Pakistan in relation to India. Europe's growing problem with its restive Muslim population was seen in the United States as evidence of Europe being less willing and able to assimilate immigrants than the United States. Perhaps most dramatically in retrospect, the United States did nothing to support the efforts of Russia (along with Iran) to prevent the Taliban from taking control of all of Afghanistan during the five years prior to 9/11. Russia and China were most in tune with each other in establishing (along with four Central Asian republics) the Shanghai Cooperation Organization just prior to 9/11 in order to combat "terrorism, separatism and extremism"—all of which Moscow and Beijing associated with Islamic radicalism. Even so, Russia's cool relations with Pakistan (which it saw as supporting Moscow's Muslim opponents in both Afghanistan and Central Asia) contrasted with China's friendly ties to Islamabad.

After 9/11, the great powers became notably more sympathetic and even more supportive of one another in many—though not all—of their different individual conflicts with various Muslim entities. European governments expressed strong support for the United States in the wake of the attack, and many contributed armed forces and other resources to the U.S.-led intervention in Afghanistan that began in October 2001. Overcoming the objections of his own defense minister, Russian president Vladimir Putin consented to the United States and some of its NATO allies making use of military facilities in former Soviet Central Asia in order to facilitate the U.S.-led intervention in Afghanistan. China (among others) voted to approve a UN Security Council Resolution in 2001 authorizing the International Security Assistance Force (ISAF) in Afghanistan, thus enhancing the legitimacy of the U.S.-led intervention. Cooperation between America and India on security issues increased significantly after

9/11, even though India was not happy about Washington's renewed reliance on Pakistan to prosecute the war in Afghanistan.

This relative degree of common purpose among the great powers with regard to Islamic radicalism, however, did not last long. The Bush administration's intervention in Iraq aroused strong opposition on the part of Russia and China, triggered serious disagreement among European Union governments, and was not well received by India. Especially in the early phases of the intervention, when it appeared to be successful, many feared that the United States would launch additional interventions and would proceed to unilaterally overthrow and replace other governments in the greater Middle East. Some polls showed that the United States was seen in many countries as more of a threat than Al Qaeda (Vogelgesang 2008). Some governments, however, opposed the U.S.-led intervention in Iraq more because they saw it as a distraction in the international struggle against Islamic radicalism. While elements of the Bush administration (particularly Vice President Cheney) insisted that Saddam Hussein and Osama bin Laden were allies, they in fact regarded each other as enemies (Bergen 2011, 132–52). The U.S.-led intervention in Iraq, which failed to establish stability there afterward, set the stage not only for Al Qaeda in Iraq and similar groups to gain a foothold in the country but also for Iran to interfere much more easily in Iraqi politics.

The global community's distrust of the United States, though, diminished as it became clear that the United States had become bogged down in a problematic military effort, both there and in Afghanistan, and that it was not likely to launch many more regime-changing interventions any time soon. Despite its being authorized by the UN Security Council, the U.S./NATO military support given to Libyan forces opposing Qaddafi in mid-2011 did not go well at first, further strengthening the view that the United States and its allies would not try this again elsewhere in the Arab world.

Despite their criticism or even opposition to them, these American-led interventions served to benefit the great power aspirations of some countries. The American presence in Afghanistan in particular has served to protect Russia and Russia's Central Asian allies from the spread of radical Islam northward into the former Soviet Union and to prevent external assistance to China's Muslim opponents in Xinjiang. Although India may not be happy about the renewal of American-Pakistani security cooperation after 9/11, American actions against the Taliban served Indian interests since the Taliban was—and still is—allied to India's rival, Pakistan. The U.S.-led intervention also opened the door to increased Indian influence in Afghanistan—something that Pakistan has not been happy about at all. Even the U.S. presence in Iraq to which they objected so strenuously has served the interests of other great powers. The award of lucrative petroleum contracts to Russian, Chinese, European, and other firms has given these countries a strong interest in the preservation of Iraq's American-sponsored government and security order. These contracts may well prove worthless if instability increases after the American military forces are withdrawn completely.

Yet at the same time as some have benefited from the American presence in Afghanistan and even Iraq, America's being distracted by these two conflicts has also benefited certain great powers. America's heavy ongoing military commitments in Iraq and Afghanistan, for example, made it virtually impossible for Washington to do much of anything to oppose the August 2008 Russian military intervention against Georgia. Similarly, it is not clear that China would have moved so aggressively to assert its claims to the South China Sea and certain islands in the East China Sea if the United States were not so bogged down in conflicts elsewhere. During the George W. Bush years, several European leaders also sought to take advantage of what they saw as America's military and moral failures to promote the great power ambitions of the European Union—especially in terms of being able to define whether or not American actions were legitimate. In addition, Brazil has taken advantage of America's preoccupation with the greater Middle East and inattention to Latin America in order to bolster its influence both in the Western Hemisphere and beyond.

As Paul Kennedy observed in *The Rise and Fall of the Great Powers* (1989), overextension on the part of one great power provides the opportunity for others to increase their relative strength. American overextension in Iraq and Afghanistan may have provided just such an opportunity to Russia, China, India, Brazil, and even the European Union.

Many Americans—especially conservatives—worry that a U.S. withdrawal from Iraq and Afghanistan will harm America's overall influence in the world. Ironically, an American withdrawal from Afghanistan in particular is likely to have much more negative consequences for Russia, China, and India. With those countries being closer to Afghanistan, the return of the Pakistani-backed Taliban will pose far more security challenges for them than it will for the United States.

▼ ▼ ▼

The Historical Context

Having stated earlier that it seems certain the War on Terror will continue for years or even decades, it may seem contradictory, premature, and even downright naive to discuss how it could end. For those who lived through it, however, the Cold War also seemed interminable and even incapable of ending. And yet it did come to a conclusion. This alone raises the possibility that what now appears to be the interminable War on Terror could also come to an end.

How might this occur? One way to examine this question is to assess the extent to which the factors that contributed to the weakening of Marxism-Leninism as a transnational revolutionary movement previously are, or may become, strong enough to contribute to the weakening of radical Islamism as a transnational revolutionary movement now.

There were three broad factors contributing to the demise of the Soviet-led Marxist-Leninist transnational revolutionary movement that could also negatively affect the radical Islamist transnational revolutionary movement: disillusion, overexpansion, and ideological competition.

Disillusion

Like Marxism-Leninism, radical Islamism appeals to many as an opposition ideology that explains their societies' problems, identifies who is responsible for them, and proposes definitive, violent solutions to overcome them. But also like Marxism-Leninism, radical Islamism has proven to be highly unappealing as a governing ideology where it has come to power. Revolutionary enthusiasm alone cannot solve a country's problems, though it can certainly compound and increase them. Nondemocratic revolutionary regimes are not inclined to accept responsibility for the failure of their misguided policies, instead blaming their failures on the machinations of internal and external enemies. Whatever idealistic goals they may have had before coming to power, their primary aim once they have done so is to remain in power—and they often prove far more ruthless and adept at doing so than the regimes they ousted. Further, while insistent on "protecting" their fellow citizens from the "corrupting influences" of Western society, the revolutionary leaders themselves usually do not deny themselves the (often conspicuous) enjoyment of these influences or of corruption generally. The result is a cynical, disillusioned citizenry that comes to oppose not only the regime but also its hollow ideology. While these disillusioned citizens are generally not strong enough to overthrow the revolutionary ruling class, they can be mobilized quickly to support its overthrow if and when it suddenly (and usually unexpectedly) becomes vulnerable—as occurred throughout Eastern Europe in 1989 and in those countries experiencing the "Arab Spring" more recently.

While radical Islamism does indeed appeal to many in countries where it helps mobilize opposition to unpopular, authoritarian regimes, there have already been strong signs of disillusion in societies where radical Islamist regimes have ruled: Iran, Sudan, and Afghanistan under the Taliban. As discussed earlier, the Taliban became so unpopular during their brief reign from 1996 to 2001 that both Pushtuns and non-Pushtuns alike joined with a relatively small number of American forces to topple them from power. Although it did not succeed in achieving its aims, the Iranian Green Movement that arose in mid-2009 (in which an astounding 2 million people took part in protest demonstrations) in reaction to the suspicious Iranian government declaration that Ahmadinejad had won reelection as president on the first ballot proved that the Islamic Republic of Iran faces serious internal opposition. In Sudan, the radical Islamist regime was so unpopular in the non-Muslim south that an overwhelming majority voted in favor of secession in the January 2011 referendum there. Indeed, Khartoum's harsh rule has also fostered a secessionist movement in the largely Muslim Darfur region. To avoid the sort of disillusion that those in Afghanistan under the Taliban, Iran, and Sudan have faced, any future radical Islamist regime will need to rule in a very different manner. But movements such as Al Qaeda, Al Qaeda in the Arabian Peninsula (or anywhere else), or the Taliban do not exhibit any signs of having learned how to avoid this problem.

Overexpansion

Transnational revolutionaries that succeed in coming to power in one country are—practically by definition—not satisfied with ruling just one country but seek to spread the "benefit" of their revolution to other countries. But as the Marxist-Leninists and later the radical Islamist regimes in Iran and Sudan learned, exporting revolution cannot be done as cheaply and as easily as the ideologues who advocate it believe. Indeed, the attempt to export revolution usually leads to one of two negative results: either it fails or, worse yet, it succeeds—but only at a prohibitive cost.

Attempting to export revolution usually elicits fierce resistance from the government whose overthrow is being sought, others who fear that they may be the next targets, one or more of the great powers (especially the United States), and perhaps others still. If those resisting the export of revolution succeed, then the resources devoted to this effort by revolutionary regimes are both wasted on a fruitless effort and diverted from (often quite urgent) domestic needs. Further, the United States in particular usually goes to considerable effort to economically isolate revolutionary regimes actively seeking to export revolution. The result of this is a loss of trade with and investment from not only America but also its allies (though their cooperation with the United States on this varies greatly). Although the revolutionary leadership may be willing to pay these costs (or even recognize them as costs), over time the diversion of their own resources abroad and limitations on economic interaction with America and the West contribute to the growth of internal disillusionment.

Successfully exporting revolution may at first appear to benefit the revolutionary regime that manages to do this, but it is frequently more costly than failing to do so. For not only does this incur the diversion of domestic resources needed to accomplish such a task and an even more vigorous effort by the United States and its allies to isolate it economically, but if the new regime it helps establish is weak, the cost of defending it can be far greater than the cost of establishing it in the first place. And if the new regime that it helped establish is not weak and does not need its help, there is absolutely no guarantee that this new regime will remain loyal to its erstwhile revolutionary mentor.

Of course, any new radical Islamist revolutionary regimes that might arise can avoid the costs of overextension simply by refraining from the attempt to export revolution. But new revolutionary regimes in particular do not usually exercise such self-restraint, as they do not foresee just how costly the attempt to export revolution will be.

Ideological Competition

One of the strengths of authoritarian transnational revolutionary movements that succeed in gaining popularity is that they espouse an ideology that many consider to be superior to others in terms of explaining their problems, proposing a solution (revolution), and promising a bright future under the rule of a particular ideology's proponents. But as noted earlier, disillusion often sets in after the proponents of a particular revolutionary ideology seize power and fail to deliver the bright future that they had promised, supplying instead only poverty, oppression, and hopelessness. It is when this happens that those who become disillusioned with the ruling revolutionary ideology may become attracted to another.

Disillusionment with Marxism-Leninism contributed to those living under it becoming attracted to Western-style democracy in much of Eastern Europe and to just plain nationalism in Russia and some other countries. Similarly, disillusionment with radical Islamism contributed to the rise of the Iranian Green Movement that seeks democratization. Of course, it is not necessary to live under the rule of a particular ideology to become disillusioned with it and attracted to another. Attacks by radical jihadists on their fellow Muslims in Iraq, Saudi Arabia, and many other countries have resulted in people there fearing radical Islamists and seeking protection from them.

Disillusion with radical Islamism, however, need not result in acquiescence to the continued rule of (often pro-Western) authoritarian regimes as the lesser of two evils. While some of the surprisingly powerful outbursts of public opposition that erupted in 2011 were targeted at regimes (more or less) allied to the United States, all of them appear to be democratically inclined "color revolution" (the term that came into popular use to describe the democratic revolutions in Georgia, Ukraine, and Kyrgyzstan in 2003, 2004, and 2005, respectively) movements and not authoritarian radical Islamist ones. While their ultimate fate is still unclear, these popular movements may succeed not only in ousting pro-Western authoritarian rulers but also in preventing radical Islamist movements from seizing power. Worst-case analysts in the West fear that radical Islamists will be able to take advantage of democratic openings in the Arab world to seize power, but worst-case analysts among the radical Islamists must fear that these popular democratic movements will forestall their hopes for establishing their own brand of authoritarian rule.

Of course, how the Cold War with the Soviet Union and its allies came to an end is not the only path by which the War on Terror might end. America and its allies were also engaged in a fierce, ideologically motivated Cold War with Communist China from 1949 until the Sino-American rapprochement of the early

1970s. This came to an end through alternate means: rifts among radicals and embourgeoisement.

Rifts among Radicals

I noted previously how rivalries between revolutionary actors can grow so intense that one or both parties to them turn to the previously reviled "imperialist" powers for support against the other. The Sino-Soviet split was the most important instance of this occurring during the Cold War era, but there were others too. Despite their common hatred for America, the West, and regimes allied to them in the Muslim world, radical Islamist actors have also developed numerous rifts among themselves during the current War on Terror era. These rifts do not usually lead to immediate rapprochements, but as they become prolonged, one or both parties to them can become more interested in—or even desperate for—rapprochement with the United States. But even if these circumstances arise, America and the West must be willing to respond positively to them for rapprochements to actually occur.

Of course, radical Islamist governments are far more likely to seek rapprochements with America and the West than radical Islamist opposition movements trying to come to power. Revolutionary governments have far more to protect and to lose than revolutionary movements do. At present, there are far more Islamic revolutionary movements seeking power than there are Islamic revolutionary regimes. The potential for rifts among radicals to lead to rapprochements with America and the West at present, then, is limited (but not nonexistent). Ironically, while more Islamic revolutionary regimes coming to power would be highly unwelcome to America and the West, their doing so offers greater potential for rifts arising among them that eventually lead to rapprochements with the United States and its allies.

Embourgeoisement

The authoritarian revolutionary leaders who first seize power are usually overly self-confident in their ability to create a revolutionary paradise in their own country and to spread their "glorious revolution" to others. They also tend to be virulently anti-American and deeply hostile to the global economic system (which they see as Western dominated and, hence, unfair to them). Very often, however, these leaders' successors, their children, or even the original leaders themselves lose confidence in their ability—or just lose the desire—to build a revolutionary paradise at home and to spread revolution elsewhere. They become far more concerned with just staying in power (much like the leaders of the regimes that they overthrew). As this more pragmatic desire becomes paramount, it often occurs to the revolutionary leadership (and especially to their children) that remaining in power—as well as personally prospering from doing so—can be achieved much more readily in cooperation with America and the West rather than in opposition to them. They decide to embrace the opportunities that the global economic system provides rather than counterproductively isolate their country from it.

Examples of this occurring during (or shortly after) the Cold War include China and Vietnam, where revolutionary regimes have remained firmly in power but have ended their previous efforts to export revolution and have embraced the global economy. Libya under Qaddafi (as well as the influence of his children) also embarked on this path, and Cuba under Fidel Castro's younger brother Raul appears to be attempting to do so. Of course, revolutionary regimes might attempt to "have their cake and eat it too," that is, have good diplomatic and trade relations with America and the West while continuing to support the radical opponents of America's allies. It is remarkable, though, how over time so many revolutionary regimes have come to see good economic and political relations with America and the West as being far more beneficial than either spreading revolution or maintaining economic isolation. It is highly doubtful that all but the most dogmatic and ascetic among the revolutionary elite in radical Islamist regimes (both present and future) are immune to the natural human greed and selfishness that have fostered embourgeoisement among their counterparts in other revolutionary regimes.

Conclusion

The factors identified here as contributing to ending the Marxist-Leninist challenge to America and the West—disillusion, over-expansion, ideological competition, rifts among radicals, and embourgeoisement—are obviously not yet strong enough to end the radical Islamist challenge to them in the near future. To a greater or lesser degree, though, these factors are either already at work in the transnational Islamic revolutionary movement or likely to become so if it expands. The radical Islamists will have to be more patient, resourceful, and foresighted while remaining more faithful to their revolutionary vision than the Marxist-Leninists were if they are to successfully avoid the corrosive effect of these five factors. And this seems—especially with the passage of time—highly unlikely.

▼ ▼ ▼

The Bush and Obama Legacies

Several parallels can be drawn between America's intervention in Indochina and its aftermath during the Cold War era on the one hand and its interventions in both Iraq and Afghanistan and their aftermath during the War on Terror era on the other.

President Kennedy initiated and President Johnson greatly expanded American military intervention in Vietnam, but the United States was unable to win this war, which subsequently became highly unpopular with the American public. Similarly, George W. Bush initiated and greatly expanded American military interventions in both Afghanistan and Iraq. The United States' inability to bring these wars to a satisfactory conclusion also resulted in their becoming highly unpopular with the American public.

Presidents Nixon and Ford oversaw America's military withdrawal from Indochina—but not before Nixon himself greatly expanded the war through launching interventions in Cambodia and Laos (from where the Vietnamese communists had previously been able to operate with impunity). Similarly, President Obama is overseeing the withdrawal of American forces from

Iraq and Afghanistan, but only after the surge in Iraq carried out at the end of the Bush years and the surge in Afghanistan undertaken by Obama.

While considered a defeat at the time, the U.S. withdrawal from Indochina under Nixon and Ford ended American overexpansion there and set up the Reagan administration in particular to more easily weaken an overexpanded Soviet Union by way of the Reagan Doctrine (aiding anti-Soviet insurgents fighting pro-Soviet Marxist-Leninist regimes in Afghanistan, Angola, Nicaragua, and elsewhere), "Star Wars" (the costly ballistic missile defense program that imposed a heavy burden on the economically weaker USSR, which tried to emulate it), and other initiatives. Similarly, while Obama's withdrawal from Iraq and Afghanistan appears to many to be inviting defeat, it may instead serve to end American overexpansion in these two countries and set up a future American president—or even Obama himself—to more easily weaken an overexpanded radical Islamist movement.

Finally, just as it seemed virtually inconceivable that democratization would sweep through Eastern Europe until after this process had gotten underway in 1989, it had seemed inconceivable that democratization could occur in the Arab world until the dramatic events of 2011 raised this possibility. It is, of course, not at all certain that the democratic revolutions that burst forth in Tunisia, Egypt, Libya, Yemen, and Syria in 2011 will actually bring democracy to these nations, much less spread it to other Arab countries. (The attempt at democratic revolution in Bahrain did not do so but was crushed instead.) Yet even if democratization does not spread or proves anemic, the mass protests resulting in the downfall of just these few Arab leaders who had been in power for decades will serve to inspire Arabs both now and in the future about what can be accomplished. Arab publics and authoritarian Arab regimes are now aware that the Arab world is not immune from the forces seeking democratic change that have spread to other regions of the world.

It cannot be predicted with any degree of certainty just how far or fast democratic revolution will occur in the Arab and the broader Muslim world. Through its support for Mubarak's resignation as president of Egypt in particular, though, the Obama administration has done more for aligning the United States with democratic change in the Arab world than the Bush administration did by calling for democratic change but then primarily backing authoritarian regimes there. If democracy takes root, in Egypt in particular, Obama's most positive legacy with regard to the War on Terror could be that he was foresighted enough to support democratic change as a means of undermining antidemocratic Islamic radicals. And even if this hoped-for democratic change does not occur, Obama's legacy will be that he brought an end to the Bush administration's overexpansion and all the problems that this caused for American foreign policy.

Furthermore, especially in light of the events of 2011, George W. Bush may also have left behind a positive legacy. To understand what this might be, we must examine a possible parallel that predates the Cold War: the legacy of Woodrow Wilson at the end of World War I.

President Wilson's vision of a peaceful, democratic Europe appeared overly optimistic and naive not just in the immediate aftermath of World War I but for several decades afterward. Yet not quite a century after the November 11, 1918, armistice, his vision has largely been fulfilled in Europe.

Why did this happen? Two key components were (1) the spread of democratic values and the discrediting of nondemocratic alternatives first in Western and later in Eastern Europe, and (2) America's commitment to supporting West European democracies after World War II (unlike after World War I) and East European democracies after the Cold War.

Similarly, Bush's support for democratization in the greater Middle East appeared overly optimistic and naive when he announced his vision for it in 2003 because the demand for democracy there appeared to be extremely weak. But the demand for democracy was also weak in much of Europe after World War I—especially after the onset of the Great Depression. This, however, did not prevent the demand for democracy from growing throughout Europe later. And American support was crucial for transforming this demand for democratization into actual democracy first in Western and later in Eastern Europe.

While the demand for democracy may have been weak in the greater Middle East up to now, Europe's experience suggests that this need not prevent it from developing later. If and when the demand for democracy does grow in the greater Middle East, American support will also be crucial for transforming it into actual democracy. But for this to happen, an American president must first be willing to acknowledge that it can happen—as President Bush was. And as has been seen in several Arab countries in 2011, there clearly is a strong demand for democracy in the greater Middle East.

Just as the Cold War era seemed unending while it was going on but did end in a surprising wave of democratization, the War on Terror era may simply prove to have been the interlude between 9/11 and 2/11—the day in 2011 when Egyptian President Mubarak resigned—and also end with a surprising wave of democratization. If so, I will leave it to others to debate whether this came about primarily because of the Bush administration's efforts, the Obama administration's, or those of individual actors within Arab and Muslim countries themselves.

Works Cited

Abdel-Latif, Omayma. 2008. "Lebanon's Sunni Islamists—A Growing Force." Carnegie Papers, no. 6. Carnegie Middle East Center. January. www.carnegieendowment.org/files/CMEC6_abdellatif_leb anon_final.pdf.

Ali, Rafid Fadhil. 2011. "Al-Qaeda in the Arabian Peninsula's Growing War with North Yemen's Houthist Movement." Jamestown Foundation Terrorism Monitor. January 14. www.jamestown.org/single /?no_cache=1&tx_ttnews%5Btt_news%5D=37363.

Arnoldy, Ben. 2010. "Why Karzai Readily Admits Receiving Bags of Iranian Cash." Christian Science Monitor, October 25. www.csmonitor .com/World/Asia-South-Central/2010/1025/Why-Karzai-readily -admits-receiving-bags-of-Iranian-cash.

Ayubi, Nazih N. 1991. Political Islam: Religion and Politics in the Arab World. London: Routledge.

Batatu, Hanna. 1978. The Old Social Classes and the Revolutionary Movements of Iraq: A Study of Iraq's Old Landed and Commercial Classes and of Its Communists, Ba'thists, and Free Officers. Princeton, NJ: Princeton University Press.

Bergen, Peter L. 2011. The Longest War: The Enduring Conflict between America and Al-Qaeda. New York: Free Press.

Black, Ian. 2011. "Al-Qaida Already Looked Irrelevant after Arab Spring."

Guardian, May 2. www.guardian.co.uk/world/2011/may/02/al-qaida
-irrelevant-arab-spring.

Blanford, Nicholas. 2011. "Hezbollah Tightens Security in Beirut Sub-
urbs." *Daily Star* (Lebanon), June 9. www.dailystar.com.lb/News
/Politics/2011/Jun-09/Hezbollah-tightens-security-in-Beirut
-suburbs.ashx#axzz1QUevfxxi.

Boucek, Christopher. 2010. "Yemen: Avoiding a Downward Spiral." In
Yemen on the Brink, edited by Christopher Boucek and Marina Ottaway, 1–30. Washington, DC: Carnegie Endowment for International Peace.

Bozorgmehr, Najmeh. 2010. "Defeated Group Returns to Haunt Iran."
Financial Times, July 16. www.ft.com/cms/s/0/4d46483e-90ce-11df
-85a7-00144feab49a.html#axzz1QULpXs80.

Brandenburg, Rachel. 2010. "Iran and the Palestinians." In *The Iran
Primer: Power, Politics, and U.S. Policy*, edited by Robin Wright, 171–74.
Washington, DC: United States Institute of Peace Press/Woodrow
Wilson International Center for Scholars.

Bull, Bartle. 2010. "The Coming Iraqi Business Boom." *Wall Street
Journal*, December 21, A19.

Bush, George W. 2003. "President Bush Discusses Freedom in Iraq and
Middle East." Remarks by the President at the 20th Anniversary of
the National Endowment for Democracy, United States Chamber
of Commerce, Washington, DC, November 6. http://georgewbush
-whitehouse.archives.gov/news/releases/2003/11/20031106-2.html.

CIA (Central Intelligence Agency). 2011. *The World Factbook*. www.cia
.gov/library/publications/the-world-factbook/index.html.

Colburn, Forrest D. 1994. *The Vogue of Revolution in Poor Countries*.
Princeton, NJ: Princeton University Press.

Cole, Juan. 2004. "Osama bin Laden's Scary Vision of a Grand Muslim Super State." History News Network, October 3. http://hnn.us
/articles/7378.html.

Dakroub, Hussein. 2011. "Hezbollah Says Major Cabinet Hurdles Re-
moved, Mikati Cautious." *Daily Star* (Lebanon), June 6. www.daily
star.com.lb/ArticlePrint.aspx?id=140479&mode=print.

Dalrymple, William. 2010. "The Military and the Mullahs." *New
Statesman*, August 23. www.newstatesman.com/asia/2010/08/india
-pakistan-afghanistan.

DeYoung, Karen, and Griff Witte. 2011. "Pakistan-U.S. Security Relationship at Lowest Point since 2001, Officials Say." *Washington Post*,
June 15. www.washingtonpost.com/national/national-security/arrest
-indicates-pakistan-leaders-face-rising-pressure-to-curb-us-role
/2011/06/12/AGrSi2VH_story.html.

Dresch, Paul. 2000. *A History of Modern Yemen*. Cambridge: Cambridge University Press.

Eickelman, Dale F. 2001. "Kings and People: Information and Authority in Oman, Qatar, and the Persian Gulf." In *Iran, Iraq, and the Arab Gulf States*, edited by Joseph A. Kechichian, 193–209. New York: Palgrave.

Eisenstadt, Michael. 2010. "Iran and Iraq." In *The Iran Primer: Power, Politics, and U.S. Policy*, edited by Robin Wright, 151–54. Washington, DC: United States Institute of Peace Press/Woodrow Wilson International Center for Scholars.

Erdbrink, Thomas. 2008. "Nine Killed at Iranian Religious Center." *Washington Post*, April 13. www.washingtonpost.com/wp-dyn/content/article/2008/04/12/AR2008041201570_pf.html.

Ewans, Martin. 2002. *Afghanistan: A Short History of Its People and Politics*. New York: Harper Perennial.

Fisher, Max. 2010. "Enemy of All States: Why Al-Qaeda Just Denounced Iran." *Atlantic*, November 11. www.theatlantic.com/international/print/2010/11/enemy-of-all-states-why-al-qaeda-just-denounced-iran/66459/.

"Fixing the Unfixable." 2010. *Economist*, August 21, 32–33.

Freedom House. 2011. "Electoral Democracies." *Freedom in the World, 2011*. New York: Freedom House. www.freedomhouse.org/uploads/fiw11/ElectoralDemocraciesFIW2011.pdf.

Gerstein, Josh, and Matt Negrin. 2011. "W.H. Changes bin Laden Account." *Politico*, May 2. www.politico.com/news/stories/0511/54162.html.

Gul, Imtiaz. 2010. *The Most Dangerous Place: Pakistan's Lawless Frontier*. New York: Viking.

Hadley, Stephen J. 2010. "The George W. Bush Administration." In *The Iran Primer: Power, Politics, and U.S. Policy*, edited by Robin Wright, 142–45. Washington, DC: United States Institute of Peace Press/Woodrow Wilson International Center for Scholars.

Haykel, Bernard. 2010. "Jihadis and the Shi'a." In *Self-Inflicted Wounds: Debates and Divisions within al-Qa'ida and Its Periphery*, edited by Assaf Moghadam and Brian Fishman, 202–23. West Point, NY: Harmony Project/Combating Terrorism Center at West Point.

Hokayem. Emile. 2010. "Iran and Lebanon." In *The Iran Primer: Power, Politics, and U.S. Policy*, edited by Robin Wright, 178–81. Washington, DC: United States Institute of Peace Press/Woodrow Wilson International Center for Scholars.

Hudson, Michael C. 1995. "Bipolarity, Rational Calculation and War in Yemen." In *The Yemeni War of 1994: Causes and Consequences*, edited by Jamal S. al-Suwaidi, 19–32. London: Saqi Books / Emirates Center for Strategic Studies and Research.

Huntington, Samuel P. 1993. *The Third Wave: Democratization in the Late Twentieth Century*. Norman: University of Oklahoma Press.

Ignatius, David. 2010. "Bringing Partners to the Fight." *Washington Post*, January 28, A25.

Jamal, Arif. 2011. "Choking Off Pakistan-U.S. Relations?" AFPAK Channel, April 15. http://afpak.foreignpolicy.com/posts/2011/04/15/choking_off_pakistan_us_relations.

Johnson, John. 2010. "Here's the New Phrase for 'War on Terror.'" *Newser*, May 20. www.newser.com/story/89500/heres-the-new-phrase-for-war-on-terror.html.

Katz, Mark N., ed. 1991. *Soviet-American Conflict Resolution in the Third World*. Washington, DC: United States Institute of Peace Press.

———. 1997. *Revolutions and Revolutionary Waves*. New York: St. Martin's Press.

———. 2009. "Obama's Approach to Russia and Iran." Middle East Strategy at Harvard, Middle East Papers no. 8, December 14. blogs.law.harvard.edu/mesh/files/2009/12/russia_iran_obama_katz.pdf.

Kennedy, Paul. 1989. *The Rise and Fall of the Great Powers: Economic Change and Military Conflict from 1500 to 2000*. New York: Vintage.

Kerr, Malcolm H. 1971. *The Arab Cold War: Gamal 'Abd al-Nasir and His Rivals, 1958–1970*, 3rd ed. New York: Oxford University Press.

Khalilzad, Zalmay, and Daniel Byman. 2000. "Afghanistan: The Consolidation of a Rogue State." *Washington Quarterly* 23(1):65–78.

La Guardia, Anton, and David Rennie. 2006. "Israel Cuts Funds as Hamas Refuses to Give Up Violence." *Telegraph*, January 31. www.telegraph.co.uk/news/worldnews/middleeast/palestinianauthority/1509328/Israel-cuts-funds-as-Hamas-refuses-to-give-up-violence.html.

Lawson, Alastair. 2011. "Pakistan's Evolving Sectarian Schism." BBC News, January 25. www.bbc.co.uk/news/world-south-asia-12278919.

Lieven, Anatol. 2011. "A Mutiny Grows in Punjab." *National Interest*, no. 112 (March–April): 15–23.

Lynch, Marc. 2010. "Jihadis and the *Ikhwan*." In *Self-Inflicted Wounds: Debates and Divisions within al-Qa'ida and Its Periphery*, edited by Assaf Moghadam and Brian Fishman, 155–82. West Point, NY: Harmony Project / Combating Terrorism Center at West Point.

Mantzikos, Ioannis. 2010. "Why the Islamic Revolution Ended: The Regional Politics of Sudan since 1989." *Mediterranean Quarterly* 21(3):46–60.

McGirk, Tim. 2010. "How Pakistani Help Gets in Karzai's Way." *Time*, March 20. www.time.com/time/world/article/0,8599,1973922,00.html.

Miller, Greg. 2011. "Bin Laden Files Show Al-Qaeda under Pressure." *Washington Post*, July 2, A1, A12.

Minority Rights Group International. 2011. *World Directory of Minorities and Indigenous Peoples.* www.minorityrights.org/directory.

Moaddel, Mansoor, Mark Tessler, and Ronald Inglehart. 2008–9. "Saddam Hussein and the Sunni Insurgency: Findings from Values Surveys." *Political Science Quarterly* 123(4):623–44.

Nader, Alireza, and Joya Laha. 2011. "Iran's Balancing Act in Afghanistan." Rand National Defense Research Institute Occasional Paper.

Nasir, Khaled. 2011. "Making Sense of the Syrian Uprising." *American Thinker*, June 5. www.americanthinker.com/2011/06/making_sense_of_the_syrian_uprising.html.

Obaid, Nawaf. 2006. "Stepping into Iraq: Saudi Arabia Will Protect Sunnis If the U.S. Leaves." *Washington Post*, November 29, A23.

"Obama's Speech in Cairo." 2009. *New York Times*, June 4. www.nytimes.com/2009/06/04/us/politics/04obama.text.html?pagewanted=print.

Page, Susan. 2011. "Poll: With bin Laden Dead, Is It Time to End War?" *USA Today*, May 10. www.usatoday.com/news/world/2011-05-10-Afghanistan-mission-bin-Laden-troops-poll_n.htm#.

"Pakistani Taliban Vow Revenge Attacks on U.S. Targets." 2011. *Dawn*, June 6. www.dawn.com/2011/06/06/pakistani-taliban-vow-revenge-attacks-on-us-targets.html.

Pape, Robert A., and James K. Feldman. 2010. *Cutting the Fuse: The Explosion of Global Suicide Terrorism and How to Stop It.* Chicago: University of Chicago Press.

Pargeter, Alison. 2011. "Are Islamist Extremists Fighting among Libya's Rebels?" *CTC Sentinel*, April 1. www.ctc.usma.edu/posts/are-islamist-extremists-fighting-among-libya%E2%80%99s-rebels.

Paz, Reuven. 2010. "Jihadis and Hamas." In *Self-Inflicted Wounds: Debates and Divisions within al-Qa'ida and Its Periphery*, edited by Assaf Moghadam and Brian Fishman, 183–201. West Point, NY: Harmony Project/Combating Terrorism Center at West Point.

Peterson, J. E. 2004. "Oman's Diverse Society: Northern Oman." *Middle East Journal* 58(1):32–51.

Phillips, Sarah. 2010. "What Comes Next in Yemen? Al-Qaeda, the Tribes, and State-Building." In *Yemen on the Brink*, edited by Christopher Boucek and Marina Ottaway, 75–89. Washington, DC: Carnegie Endowment for International Peace.

Pollock, David, and Ahmed Ali. 2010. "Iran Gets Negative Reviews in Iraq, Even from Shiites." Washington Institute for Near East Policy, PolicyWatch no. 1653, May 4. www.washingtoninstitute.org /templateCo5.php?CID=3199.

Risen, James. 1998. "Russians Are Back in Afghanistan, Aiding Rebels." *New York Times*, July 27. www.nytimes.com/1998/07/27/world /russians-are-back-in-afghanistan-aiding-rebels.html?pagewanted =print&src=pm.

———. 2010. "U.S. Identifies Vast Mineral Riches in Afghanistan." *New York Times*, June 13. www.nytimes.com/2010/06/14/world/asia /14minerals.html.

Rodman, Peter W. 1994. *More Precious than Peace: The Cold War and the Struggle for the Third World*. New York: Charles Scribner's Sons.

Rosenberg, Matthew, and Habib Zahori. 2010. "Karzai Slams the West Again." *Wall Street Journal*, April 4. http://online.wsj.com/article /SB10001424052702303917304575162012382865940.html.

Scahill, Jeremy. 2011. "The Dangerous US Game in Yemen." *Nation*, March 30. www.thenation.com/article/159578/dangerous-us-game -yemen.

Schmitt, Eric, Thom Shanker, and David E. Sanger. 2011. "U.S. Was Braced for Fight with Pakistanis in bin Laden Raid." *New York Times*, May 9. www.nytimes.com/2011/05/10/world/asia/10intel.html.

Shafi, Kamran. 2010. "Defining 'Strategic Depth.'" *Dawn*, January 19. http://archives.dawn.com/archives/152202.

Shermatova, Sanobar. 2001. "Massoud between Moscow and Europe." *Moskovskiye novosti*, no. 17. English translation in *Current Digest of the Post-Soviet Press*, 53(18):7.

Sly, Liz. 2011. "Arab Response to bin Laden's Death Muted." *Washington Post*, May 2. www.washingtonpost.com/world/war-zones/arab -response-to-bin-ladens-death-muted/2011/05/02/AF69WLcF _story.html.

Solomon, Jay. 2009. "U.S. Drops 'War on Terror' Phrase, Clinton Says." *Wall Street Journal*, March 31. http://online.wsj.com/article /SB123845123690371231.html.

"South Yemen Tribes Turn against Qaeda Allies." 2011. *Khaleej Times*, July 17. www.khaleejtimes.com/displayarticle.asp?xfile=data/middle east/2011/July/middleeast_July389.xml&section=middleeast&col=.

Stookey, Robert W. 1978. *Yemen: The Politics of the Yemen Arab Republic*. Boulder, CO: Westview Press.

Telhami, Shibley. 2001. "Camp David II: Assumptions and Consequences." *Current History* 100(642):10–14.

Vogelgesang, Sandy. 2008. "Perspectives on Public Diplomacy: Vietnam to Iraq." *Fletcher Forum of World Affairs* 32(3):101–10.

Walt, Stephen M. 1996. *Revolution and War.* Ithaca, NY: Cornell University Press.

Weinbaum, Marvin G. 1991. "War and Peace in Afghanistan: The Pakistani Role." *Middle East Journal* 45(1):71–85.

Wilson, Scott, and Al Kamen. 2009. "'Global War on Terror' Is Given New Name." *Washington Post*, March 25. www.washingtonpost.com/wp-dyn/content/article/2009/03/24/AR2009032402818_pf.html.

Winter, Lucas. 2011. "Conflict in Yemen: Simple People, Complicated Circumstances." *Middle East Policy* 18(1):121–31.

Woodward, Bob. 2010. *Obama's Wars.* New York: Simon and Schuster.

Yamani, Mai. 2008. "The Two Faces of Saudi Arabia." *Survival* 50(1): 143–56.

Zaboun, Kifah. 2010. "Hamas-Islamic Jihad Relations Deteriorating." *Asharq Alawsat*, August 29. www.asharq-e.com/news.asp?section=1&id=22135.

Index

About the Author

Mark N. Katz is a professor of government and politics at George Mason University in Fairfax, VA, and a nonresident senior fellow at the Middle East Policy Council in Washington, DC. He writes on Russian foreign policy, the international relations of the Middle East, and transnational revolutionary movements. He is the author of *The Third World in Soviet Military Thought* (Johns Hopkins University Press, 1982), *Russia and Arabia: Soviet Foreign Policy toward the Arabian Peninsula* (Johns Hopkins University Press, 1986), *Gorbachev's Military Policy in the Third World* (Center for Strategic and International Studies, 1989), *Revolutions and Revolutionary Waves* (St. Martin's Press, 1997), and *Reflections on Revolutions* (St. Martin's Press, 1999). He is also the editor of *The USSR and Marxist Revolutions in the Third World* (Woodrow Wilson International Center for Scholars/Cambridge University Press, 1990), *Soviet-American Conflict Resolution in the Third World* (United States Institute of Peace Press, 1991), and *Revolution: International Dimensions* (CQ Press, 2001).

Links to many of his publications can be found on his website: www.marknkatz.com.